The Official Guide to

Family Tree Maker

VERSION 11

The Official Guide to

Family Tree Maker®

VERSION 11

Rhonda R. McClure

MyFamily.com™

Library of Congress Cataloging-in-Publication Data

McClure, Rhonda R.
  The official guide to family tree maker, version 11 / by Rhonda R.
McClure.
      p. cm.
Includes index.
  ISBN 1-59331-039-0 (pbk. : alk. paper)
  1. Family tree maker. 2. Genealogy—Computer programs. 3.
Genealogy—Data processing. I. Title.
  CS14.M349 2003
  929'.1'0285536—dc22

                                            2003016170

Published by MyFamily.com, Inc.

P.O. Box 990

Orem, UT 84059

10 9 8 7 6 5 4 3 2 1

Printed in the United States of America

For Marie and Michael; you made this possible.

Table of Contents

Introduction xv

Part I   ***Introduction to Family Tree Maker***...1
Chapter 1   **Getting Started with Family Tree Maker**..3
                 Starting Family Tree Maker 4
                 Creating a New Family File 5

Chapter 2   **Getting to Know Family Tree Maker**..13
                 Exploring Family Tree Maker 14
                 Navigating the Fields 18
                 Understanding the Different Views 19
                 Moving Information 27
                 Exiting Family Tree Maker 28

Chapter 3   **Family Tree Maker for Beginners** 29
                 Entering a Primary Individual 30
                 Entering an Event 31
                 Changing the Date Format 33
                 Adding Individuals 35
                 Adding an Additional Spouse 38
                 Moving a Child to the Primary Individual Position 43

Part II   ***Using Family Tree Maker Features***...45
Chapter 4   **Enhancing the Family**...47
                 Adding Parents..48
                 Working with Children 50
                 Arranging Child Order 55

Chapter 5   **Documenting Sources** 63
Where Can You Cite Sources? 64
Citing a Source 64
Attaching Images to Sources 80

Chapter 6   **Understanding More About Options** 83
Working with the More About Facts Window 84
Using the Address Window 89
Working with Medical Information 91
Opening the More About Lineage Window 93

Chapter 7   **Using More About Notes** 97
Working with Notes and Stories 98
Finding Text in Notes 105
Importing Text to Notes 108
Exporting Notes 111
Formatting Notes for Printing 112

Chapter 8   **Working with More About Marriage** 115
Accessing the More About Marriage Window 116
Using the More About Marriage Facts Window 116
Working with Marriage Notes 121

Chapter 9   **Getting into Individual Facts Cards** 123
Accessing the Individual Facts Card 124
Individual Facts Card Versus the Family Page 125
Working with the Individual Facts Card 128

Part III   **Working in Family Tree Maker** 135
Chapter 10   **Searching Your Family Tree File** 137
Using Quick Search by Name 138
Working with the Find Feature 139
Rearranging the Index 141
Using the Find Individual Feature 144
Working with the FamilyFinder Center 152

Chapter 11   **Correcting Information in Family Tree Maker**.....................157
Working with the Family Tree Maker Spelling Checker 158
Untying the Marriage Knot 161
Removing People from Your Family File 163
Checking the Family File for Errors 166

Chapter 12   **Fixing Relationships & Duplicates**................................173
Fixing Relationships 174
Fixing Duplicates 181
Using Global Find and Replace 189

Part IV   **Getting to Know Family Tree Maker Trees and Reports**.191
Chapter 13   **Looking at the Tree Reports in Family Tree Maker**.......193
Displaying Ancestor Trees 194
Displaying Hourglass Trees 204
Displaying Descendant Trees 206
Displaying All-in-One Trees 209
Enhancing Tree Views 211

Chapter 14   **Working with Specialty Reports and the Research Journal**......217
Creating a Custom Report 218
Exporting Reports to a Spreadsheet 226
Creating a Kinship Report 227
Working with Address and Birthday Reports 228
Using the Research Journal 230
Adding a To-Do Item Anytime 235

Chapter 15   **Viewing and Printing Reports and Trees**.......................237
Viewing the Tree You Want to Print 238
Customizing the View 238
Printing the Tree 242
Saving the Tree in PDF Format 244

Chapter 16   **Creating Genealogy Style and Genealogical Source Reports**...245
Using Genealogy Style Reports 246
Using Endnotes 251

Formatting the Report 252

Locating Conflicting Facts 255

Creating a Bibliography Report 257

Creating a Documented Events Report 258

Part V **Publishing Your Family History** 261

Chapter 17 **Creating a Scrapbook** 263

Using the Scrapbook 264

Inserting Scrapbook Objects 265

Entering Information about Scrapbook Objects 270

Rearranging Scrapbook Objects 272

Enhancing Your Images 275

Searching for Objects 279

Sharing Your Scrapbook 281

Chapter 18 **Creating a Family History Book** 285

Selecting Available Items 286

Working with Outline Items 293

Finalizing the Book 295

Sharing Your Book 298

Chapter 19 **Creating Your Personal Family Tree Maker Home Page**......303

Creating Your First Home Page 304

Working with Your Home Page 309

Removing Items from Your Home Page 316

Part VI **Advanced Family Tree Maker Methods** 321

Chapter 20 **Working with Dates and Facts** 323

Working with the Marriage Fact 324

Removing a Custom Fact Name 329

Calculating Dates or Ages 335

Chapter 21 **Working with GEDCOM Files and Other Family Files**.........337

Creating a GEDCOM File 338

Opening Two Family Files 352

Saving a Backup of Your Family File 356

Chapter 22 **Working with Family Tree Maker Preferences** 361

Changing Family Tree Maker Preferences 362

Protecting Privacy 368

Customizing the Toolbar 370

Family File Statistics 372

Chapter 23 **Enhancing Your Family History Book** 375

Preparing Reports in Advance 376

Renaming Outline Items 382

Adding Place Holders 384

Adding to a Book 385

Part VII ***Appendixes*** 393

Chapter A **Installing Family Tree Maker** 395

Uninstalling Family Tree Maker 399

Chapter B **Using Keyboard Shortcuts** 401

Learning the Keyboard Shortcuts 402

Working with Text 403

Glossary 405

Index 411

About the Author 419

Acknowledgments

A book is a group effort. While the author comes up with the original concept and begins to bring that concept to life, there are many others who help along the way before that book becomes a finished project. Without the help and input of many talented people, this book would not be the work you are holding today. To Jennifer Utley, thank you for the chance to work with you and Ancestry. Thanks to Matt Wright for working with me on this project; it was nice to work with you again. Special thanks to Myra Vanderpool Gormley for her willingness to act as tech editor despite her own busy schedule.

Introduction

This guidebook will help you learn Family Tree Maker 11 quickly, leaving you more time for researching your family history and requiring less time for learning how to enter it into a computer program. Family Tree Maker is a multifaceted program, useful not only for tracking your ancestry, but also of producing beautiful reports and books when you wish to share what you have found. Even if you have never used a genealogy program before, you will find that Family Tree Maker's interface and options make it possible to keep track of even the most tangled of family trees. With the added capability to include digitized images, Family Tree Maker gives you the opportunity to share more than just dry names, dates, and places. This book introduces you to many of the features available in Family Tree Maker so you can enjoy this hobby you've discovered. If you have used Family Tree Maker before, you may find some new tricks in the Advanced Methods section.

Who Should Read This Book?

This book is written with the novice computer user in mind. In it, you are taken on a hands-on trip through the Family Tree Maker program. The many illustrations let you check your progress as you master each new feature or process. Even if you are familiar with computers, though, you may have only recently been introduced to Family Tree Maker. In either case, this book offers you an easy-to-follow tour of the program and all that you can accomplish. As you compare your own screen to the screen captures in the book you will be able to see if you are using the program correctly. Finally, those who feel comfortable with the basic features of Family Tree Maker may find some shortcuts or new methods for working with the program, especially in the Advanced Methods section.

This book is organized by tasks. Some tasks may require many steps, and others may branch off into enhancements or additional features. A quick perusal of the Table of

Contents should lead you right to the process you are trying to accomplish. Then it is just a matter of reading through the steps.

Special Features of This Book

As you work with this book, you will discover that the emphasis is on tasks. This is by design, so that you can master what you need in an easy-to-follow format. There are a couple of features, though, that will supply you with additional information as you work with the Family Tree Maker program.

Tips offer you useful hints about features in Family Tree Maker that can speed up the task at hand or enhance your report output.

Notes offer additional information about Family Tree Maker or about genealogy and sharing your family tree.

In the appendixes you will find help for installing the Family Tree Maker software and useful tables of keyboard shortcuts to make your data entry speedier.

Happy family tree climbing!

PART

I

Introduction to Family Tree Maker

Chapter 1
Getting Started with Family Tree Maker 3

Chapter 2
Getting to Know Family Tree Maker 13

Chapter 3
Family Tree Maker for Beginners 29

1

Getting Started with Family Tree Maker

Before you can take advantage of the many features of this program, you must know how to launch or open it. Be sure to have some of your family history information ready to enter so that you can begin to see how the program handles your family data. Family Tree Maker offers different methods for both opening the program and beginning a new Family File. In this chapter, you'll learn how to:

- Start Family Tree Maker using the Start Menu
- Start Family Tree Maker using the desktop icon
- Enter information using the Family Tree Maker wizard
- Begin your Family File using the Family Page

Starting Family Tree Maker

When Family Tree Maker was installed (see Appendix A, "Installing Family Tree Maker"), the installation set up two different ways for you to launch the Family Tree Maker program.

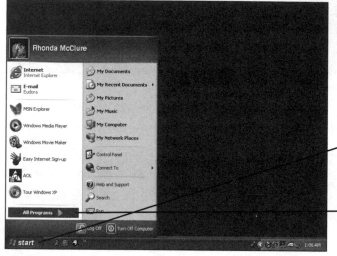

Launching Family Tree Maker from the Menu

For each program installed on your computer, there is a Start Menu option that allows you to launch the program. Family Tree Maker is no different.

1. Click on the **Start button** on the Windows Taskbar. The Start menu will appear.

2. Move the **mouse pointer** to Programs (or **All Programs** in Windows XP). The Programs menu will appear.

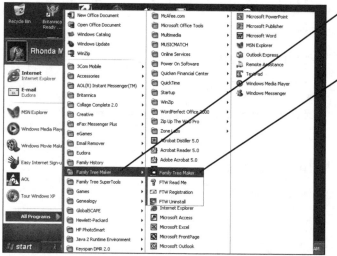

3. Move the **mouse pointer** to **Family Tree Maker**. The Family Tree Maker menu will appear.

4. Click on **Family Tree Maker**. Family Tree Maker will start.

Launching Family Tree Maker from the Desktop

Family Tree Maker installs an icon on the Windows desktop that saves you time and steps by taking you directly to the Family Tree Maker program.

1. **Double-click** on the **Family Tree Maker icon**. Family Tree Maker will start.

> ### NOTE
>
> The desktop in Windows is the main screen you see when you boot up your computer. This screen often has icons for different programs you have installed as well as other items that were installed by Windows the first time you turned on the computer.

Creating a New Family File

The first step to using Family Tree Maker is to enter information about your family. For most of us, this means taking the bits and pieces of family information gathered over the years and entering it into the program.

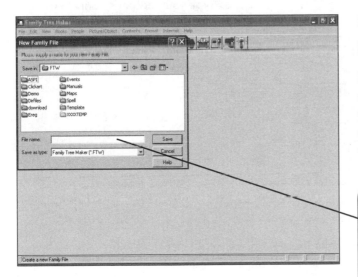

Using the Family Tree Maker Wizard

Family Tree Maker offers an easy introduction to help you enter data about yourself and your family. When you create a new family file, a wizard appears to help you enter information.

> ### NOTE
>
> Family Tree Maker will prompt you for a file name for your new Family File. After you type a file name in the File name field, just click on the Save button.

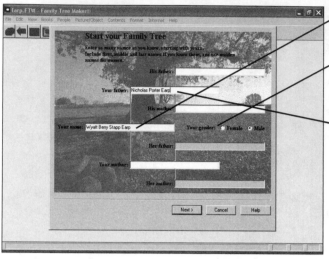

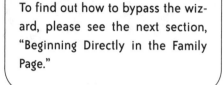

1. Type your **name** in the **Your name** field.

2. Click on the appropriate **gender radio button**. The gender will be selected.

3. Click in the **Your father field** and **enter** your **father's name**.

> **NOTE**
>
> To find out how to bypass the wizard, please see the next section, "Beginning Directly in the Family Page."

4. Press the **Tab key**. The cursor will move to the Your mother field.

5. Type your **mother's name** in the Your mother field.

6. Press the **Tab key**. The cursor will move to the His father field.

> **TIP**
>
> When using the Start Your Family Tree wizard, you must enter at least three names. You will likely know your and your parents' information best.

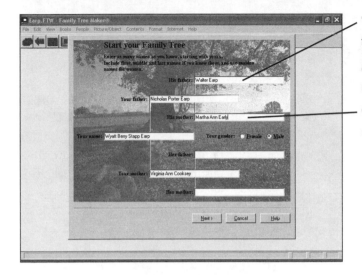

7. Type the **name** of your father's father in the His father field.

8. Press the **Tab key.** The cursor will move to the His mother field.

9. Type the **name** of your father's mother in the His mother field.

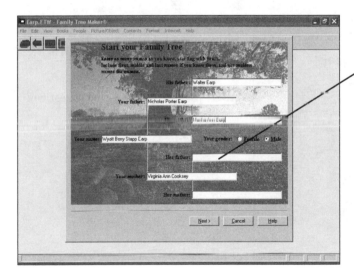

10. Press the **Tab key**. The cursor will move to the Her father field.

11. Type the **name** of your mother's father In the Her father field.

12. Press the **Tab key.** The cursor will move to the Her mother field.

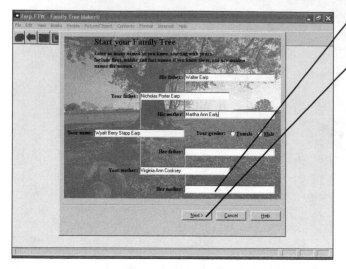

13. Type the **name** of your mother's mother in the Her mother field.

14. Click on the **Next button**. The Births screen will appear.

NOTE

Don't worry if you don't know all this information. Fill in as much as you can so that you'll have some information to work with.

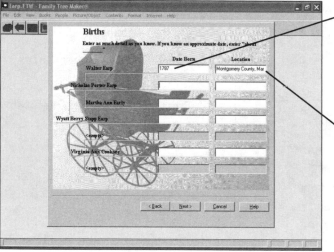

15. In the Date Born field, **enter** the **date of birth** for the first person in the Births window.

16. Press the **Tab key**. The cursor will move to the Location field.

17. Type the **place of birth** for that person.

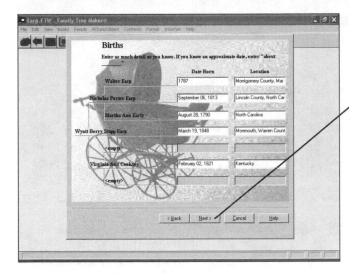

18. Press the **Tab key** to work through the remaining individuals in the Births screen and **enter** any known **birth-places and dates of birth**.

19. Click on the **Next button**. The Deaths window will appear.

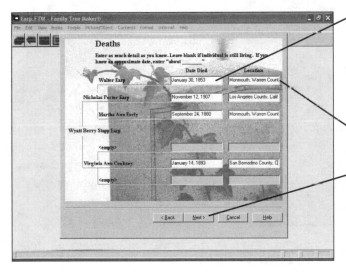

20. In the **Date Died** field, **type** the **date of death** for the first person in the Deaths window.

21. Press the **Tab key** The cursor will move to the Location field.

22. Enter the **place of death** for that person.

23. Click on the **Next button** when you have finished entering death information for each person. The FamilyFinder Search window will appear.

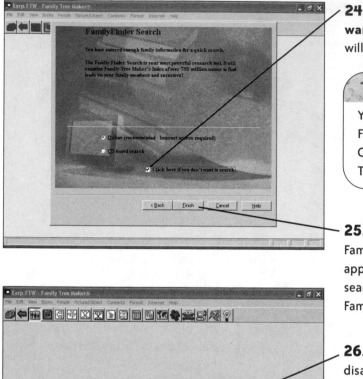

24. **Click** on the **Click here if you don't want to search check box**. The option will be selected.

NOTE

You will be introduced to the FamilyFinder search and report in Chapter 10, "Searching Your Family Tree File."

25. **Click** on the **Finish button**. A Family Tree Maker message box will appear, telling you that you can run a search any time by clicking on the FamilyFinder icon.

26. **Click** on **OK**. The message box will disappear.

TIP

If the Cue Card appears, press the Escape key to close it. For more information on the Cue Card, see Chapter 2, "Understanding Family Tree Maker."

Beginning Directly in the Family Page

The best way to get some of your initial information into the program is by using the wizard since it guides you through the initial entry. You can, however, bypass the wizard and begin entering information directly into the Family Page in Family Tree Maker. The second time you open the file, and on all subsequent sessions, you will be brought directly to the Family Page of the last Individual viewed before FTM was closed.

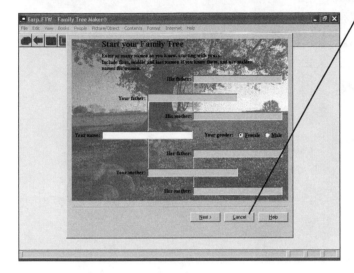

1. Click on the **Cancel button**. A message box will appear, asking you whether you want to go to the Family Page.

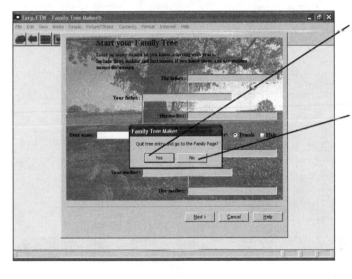

2a. Click on **Yes** The message box will disappear and you will go directly to the Family Page.

OR

2b. Click on **No**. The message box will disappear and you will go back to the wizard.

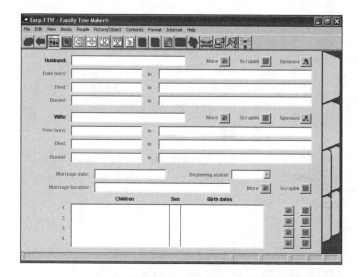

3. Click on **OK** in the Cue Card. The Cue Card will disappear.

Building from Another Person's Research

You may be one of those fortunate enough to have family members who have already been researching your family tree. If they are willing to share, you will want to ask them to send you a GEDCOM (GEnealogical Data COMmunication) file. Family Tree Maker can import this file into your Family File. See Chapter 21, "Working with GEDCOM Files and Other Family Files," for more information.

2

Getting to Know Family Tree Maker

Learning any new software program requires an introduction to its interface. There are usually some new menu items, push buttons, and choices that are specific to the program. This is true of Family Tree Maker, and this chapter introduces you to those items. In this chapter, you'll learn how to:

- Execute commands with menus and toolbars
- Use dialog boxes and scroll bars
- Navigate the various Family Page fields
- Select different views
- Move information
- Exit Family Tree Maker

Exploring Family Tree Maker

As you look at the Family Tree Maker screen, you will see a number of buttons and tabs. These buttons allow you to perform the different tasks in the program. The tabs allow you to maneuver through your family history database. This section introduces you to these features.

Using Menus

Menus are lists of the functions built into software programs. As in most software programs, the Family Tree Maker menus are activated by clicking on the words that appear along the top bar of the Family Tree Maker program window. Each menu contains a list of related commands.

1. Click on a **menu** name. The menu you chose will appear.

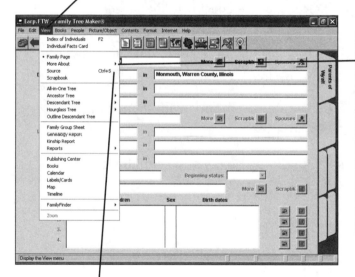

NOTE

If a menu command is followed by a right-pointing arrow, another menu will appear when you move the mouse pointer to that menu option. If a menu command is grayed out, it means that the command is not currently available. You might need to perform some other action or switch to a different view in order to activate the grayed-out command.

TIP

Some menu commands have keyboard shortcuts. You will find the keyboard shortcuts listed to the right of the menu command. You can use these shortcuts to execute commands, rather than using the menus. To learn about some of the most popular keyboard shortcuts, see Appendix B, "Using Keyboard Shortcuts."

2. Move the **mouse pointer** over a menu item with a right-pointing arrow. A second menu will appear.

3. Move the **mouse pointer** over an option on the second menu. The menu item will be highlighted.

NOTE

Click on a menu option to execute that command. This might change the view of the screen, open a dialog box requesting additional information or choices, or open another window.

Using Toolbars

There is one toolbar in Family Tree Maker. The toolbar offers buttons to access some of the more popular views, as well as a few shortcut buttons to some of the unique commands.

1. Move the **mouse pointer** over each of the toolbar buttons. The name of the function of that toolbar button will appear in a small pop-up window.

2. Click on the **Family Page button** on the toolbar. The Family Page window will appear.

NOTE

When you click on the various toolbar buttons or make certain menu choices, Family Tree Maker will open a Cue Card. The Cue Card offers some tips for working with that option.

TIP

If you do not wish to see the Cue Cards, you can turn them off. Click on the Click here if you don't want to see this Help Window again check box, then click on the OK button. To learn more about turning this feature on and off, see Chapter 22, "Working with Family Tree Maker Preferences."

Understanding Dialog Boxes

In Family Tree Maker, dialog boxes allow you to make choices and select additional options. They also allow you to select items or preferences. Before you work with the example in this section, be sure you are in the Family Page view, which is the default screen in Family Tree Maker, and that you're working with a family that has both a husband and a wife.

1. Click on the **People menu**. The menu will appear.

2. Click on **Other Spouses**. The Other Spouses dialog box will open.

TIP

You can also access the Other Spouses dialog box by pressing the F3 key. See Chapter 3 "Family Tree Maker for Beginners" for more information on using the Other Spouses options.

Moving around with Scroll Bars

In Family Tree Maker, scroll bars are found at the right and at the bottom of windows, where the text or report extends beyond the limits of the window. There are three different ways to move up and down or sideways using the scroll bars.

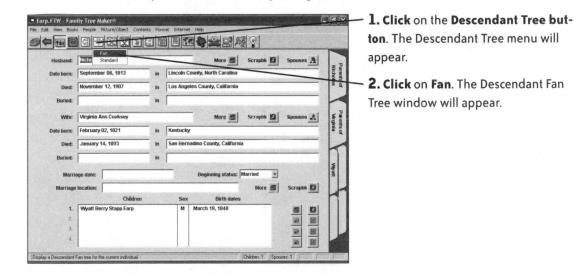

1. Click on the **Descendant Tree button**. The Descendant Tree menu will appear.

2. Click on **Fan**. The Descendant Fan Tree window will appear.

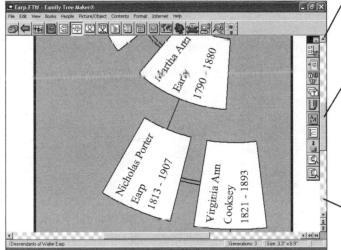

- **Click** on the **arrow** at either end of the vertical (or horizontal) scroll bar. This will scroll the page up or down (or side to side) one line at a time.

- **Press and hold** the **mouse button** on the vertical (or horizontal) scroll box and **drag** the **scroll box** up or down (or side to side) within the scroll bar. This allows you to move through more of the page at a time.

- **Click** inside the **vertical (or horizontal) scroll bar**. This moves the page up or down (or side to side) one screen at a time.

Navigating the Fields

When you work in the main entry screens of Family Tree Maker, you will need to jump from field to field to enter the appropriate information. Since much of what is taking place at this time is done on the keyboard, keyboard commands are the easiest way to do this.

1. Click on the **Family Page button**. The Family Page window will appear.

2. Navigate through the **fields** using one of the following methods:

- **Press** the **Tab key** to move from one field to another within the Family Page view.

- **Press** the **Enter key** to move from one field to another within the Family Page view.

- **Press** the **up arrow or down arrow** to move from one field to another within the Family Page view.

As you move through the fields, each field that the cursor arrives at will be highlighted.

NOTE

When you navigate in the Family Page view using any of the keyboard commands, you will notice that you move from one field to the next where typing is allowed. Family Tree Maker will bypass any other options on the page.

3. Type some new **information** in one of the fields. The highlighted field's information will change.

CAUTION

You do not want to use this method to change the order of children. Do not simply highlight the child in question and type the name of the new child. Doing this simply changes the name of the already entered individual; it does not rearrange the children. Methods of rearranging children are examined in Chapter 4, "Enhancing the Family."

Understanding the Different Views

Family Tree Maker offers different views to display your family data. Some of these views are limited to a single-family unit, while others display multigenerational charts of ancestors, descendants, or both.

Exploring the Family Page

The Family Page view is where you will spend the most time. This is where you'll enter much of your data and where you'll access the other areas in which data can be entered.

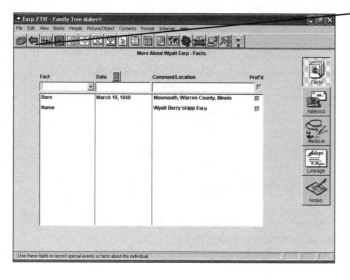

1. Click on the **Family Page button**. The Family Page will appear.

2. Click on the **More button**. The More About window will appear.

3. Click on the **Go Back button**. The Family Page will appear.

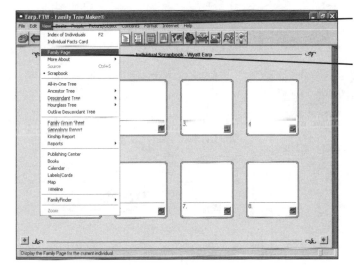

4. Click on the **Scrapbk button**. The Individual Scrapbook window will appear.

5. Click on **View**. The View menu will appear.

6. Click on **Family Page**. The Family Page will appear.

7. Click on the **Spouses button**. The Spouses of dialog box will open.

> **NOTE**
>
> You will work more closely with the Spouses of dialog box in Chapter 3, "Family Tree Maker for Beginners."

Looking at the Individual Facts Card

The Individual Facts Card offers you everything you can access through the Family Page buttons in one easy-to-use window, complete with tabs and options.

1. Click on **View**. The View menu will appear.

2. Click on **Individual Fact Card**. The Individual Facts Card window will appear.

> **NOTE**
>
> When you are in the Family Page, the only way to access the Individual Facts Card is through the View menu.

NOTE

To learn how to work with the Individual Facts Card, see Chapter 9, "Getting into Individual Facts Cards."

Working with the Ancestor Tree

The Ancestor Tree view offers a chart of the ancestors of a selected individual. There are three different formats in which to display this information.

1. Click on the **Ancestor Tree button**. The Ancestor Tree menu will appear.

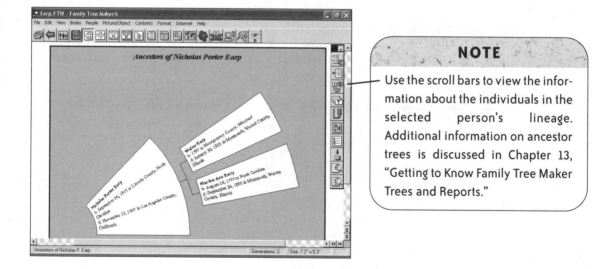

2a. Click on **Fan**. The Fan Chart will appear.

OR

2b. Click on **Standard**. The Standard Ancestor Tree will appear.

OR

2c. Click on **Vertical**. The Vertical Ancestor Tree will appear.

OR

2d. Click on **Standard Pedigree Tree**. The Standard Pedigree Tree will appear.

NOTE

Use the scroll bars to view the information about the individuals in the selected person's lineage. Additional information on ancestor trees is discussed in Chapter 13, "Getting to Know Family Tree Maker Trees and Reports."

Working with the Descendant Tree

The Descendant Tree view offers a chart of the descendants of a selected individual. There are two different formats in which you can display this information.

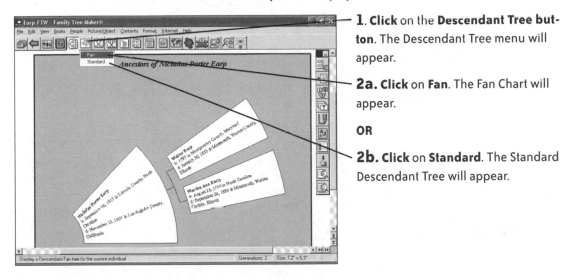

1. Click on the **Descendant Tree button**. The Descendant Tree menu will appear.

2a. Click on **Fan**. The Fan Chart will appear.

OR

2b. Click on **Standard**. The Standard Descendant Tree will appear.

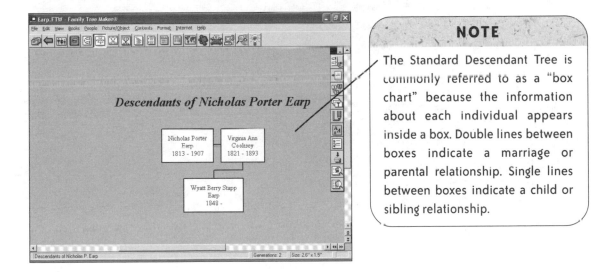

NOTE

The Standard Descendant Tree is commonly referred to as a "box chart" because the information about each individual appears inside a box. Double lines between boxes indicate a marriage or parental relationship. Single lines between boxes indicate a child or sibling relationship.

Working with the Hourglass Tree

The Hourglass Tree view offers a chart of both the descendants and ancestors of a selected individual. There are two different formats in which you can display this information.

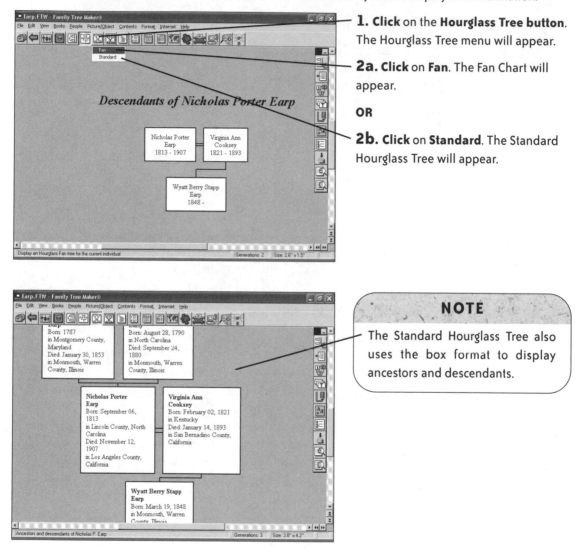

1. Click on the **Hourglass Tree button**. The Hourglass Tree menu will appear.

2a. Click on **Fan**. The Fan Chart will appear.

OR

2b. Click on **Standard**. The Standard Hourglass Tree will appear.

NOTE

The Standard Hourglass Tree also uses the box format to display ancestors and descendants.

Moving Information

Family Tree Maker allows you to use the standard Windows Copy and Paste functions to move information from field to field.

1. Place the **mouse pointer** in front of the first character you want to select and **click and drag** the **pointer** until you reach the last character you wish to cut or copy. The selected text will be high-lighted.

2. Click on **Edit**. The Edit menu will appear.

3a. Click on **Cut Text**. The selected text will be placed on the Clipboard.

OR

3b. Click on **Copy**. The Copy sub-menu will appear, and you can select the Copy Text option.

NOTE

The Cut Text command removes the text from the highlighted field and places it on the clipboard. The Copy Text command leaves the text in the highlighted field and creates a copy on the Clipboard.

4. Click in the **field** where you want to paste the information.

5. Click on **Edit**. The Edit menu will appear.

6. Click on **Paste Text**. The copied (or cut) text will appear in the field you selected.

Exiting Family Tree Maker

You have now seen the basics of the Family Tree Maker program. When you have finished your session, you will want to close the program.

1. Click on **File**. The File menu will appear.

2. Click on **Exit**. Family Tree Maker will close.

TIP

You can also close the program by clicking the Close button (X) in the upper-right corner of the Family Tree Maker window.

3 Family Tree Maker for Beginners

You will spend much of your time in Family Tree Maker entering the data you have uncovered about your family. At first, this information will likely focus on yourself, your parents, and perhaps your grandparents. Eventually, however, you will likely find yourself with ancestral lines that go back many generations. Family Tree Maker helps you keep all of this information straight. In this chapter, you'll learn how to:

- Enter a primary individual

- Enter an event

- Change the date format

- Add a spouse

- Add children

- Add an additional spouse

- Move a child to the primary individual position

Entering a Primary Individual

Family Tree Maker allows you to record the information for each individual in your family history. In the Family Page view you enter specific information for the husband, wife, and children.

1. Type the **husband's name** in the Husband field.

NOTE

The primary individual can be entered in either the **Husband** field or the **Wife** field, depending on his or her gender.

TIP

An individual's name is made up of given names (first and middle names) and the surname (last name), typed in that order.

2. Press the **Tab key**. The cursor will move to the Date born field.

NOTE

Notice that when the Tab key is pressed, the options to the right of the husband's name are bypassed. These features are accessed by clicking on them or by pulling down the appropriate menu item.

Understanding Names in Family Tree Maker

Generally, when entering the name of an ancestor in Family Tree Maker, you will simply type the name (as it appears in the record or resource you are viewing) directly into the **Name** field in Family Tree Maker's Family Page. However, there are a few instances where the surname (last name) is not just a single word. In such instances, it is necessary to identify the surname for Family Tree Maker. This is done by surrounding the surname with backward slashes (\). There are many different reasons that a surname may be more than one word. This is especially true in the research of European names. Here are some examples, with the backward slash mark included, to give you an idea of what such a name should look like:

George \de la Vergne\

Peter \Van Der Voort\

Pierre \Bourbeau dit Lacourse\

Teresa \Garcia Ramirez\

Another instance in which you might need to use backward slashes is when entering someone who does not have a last name, such as a person of Native American descent. For instance, your ancestor might have been known as Running Bear. This name would be entered in Family Tree Maker as Running Bear\\.

Parents: Virginia and Nicholas Earp

Entering an Event

When you record your family history, you must concentrate on names, dates, and places. Therefore, Family Tree Maker includes these basic fields in the Family Page view.

1. Type a **date** in the Date born field.

NOTE

There is a way to calculate dates in Family Tree Maker. See "Calculating Dates and Ages" in Chapter 20 "Working with Dates and Facts."

2. **Press** the **Tab key**. The cursor will move to the next field.

> **TIP**
>
> The traditional method for recording dates is to enter the numerals of the day, followed by the first three letters of the month, followed by the full four numerals of the year. Family Tree Maker defaults to a different setting. You'll learn how to change this setting later in this chapter, in the "Changing the Date Format" section.

3. If known, **type** a **birth location** in the in field.

4. **Press** the **Tab key**. The cursor will move to the next field.

> **NOTE**
>
> When you enter the place name, use commas to separate the different divisions. Places should always be entered from smallest division, such as a town, to largest division, such as a state or country. Generally the country is omitted when it is the United States.

5. **Type** a **date** in the Died field, if known.

6. **Press** the **Tab key**. The cursor will move to the in field.

7. Type a **location** in the in field, if known.

Changing the Date Format

As was mentioned earlier, Family Tree Maker's default setting for dates is different than the standard followed in the genealogical community. If you plan to exchange your Family Tree Maker file with others, you may want to change this setting.

1. Click on **File**. The File menu will appear.

2. Click on **Preferences**. The Preferences dialog box will open.

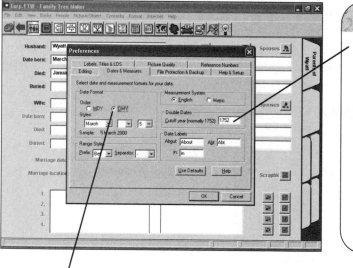

3. Click on the **Dates & Measures** tab. The Dates & Measures options will appear.

In the Dates & Measures dialog box, you can set the cutoff date for double dating. Double dating was the result of the change from the Julian to the Gregorian calendar. The Gregorian calendar determined that January would be the first month of the year. This took place for England, one of the last countries to change, and its colonies in 1752.

4. Choose the **DMY option** to conform to standard genealogical dating. The option will be selected.

5. Select the **Month style** from the Styles drop-down list. The standard method is to use the first three letters of the month.

> ### TIP
>
> Similar drop-down lists are available for changing the separator between the day, month, and year, and also for the format of the names of each day.

6. **Click** on **OK**. The Dates & Measures dialog box will close.

> ### NOTE
>
> The selections made in the **Dates & Measures** dialog box will automatically take effect in the **Family Page** screen.

Adding Individuals

The longer you research your family history the more names, dates, and places you will find. Programs like Family Tree Maker help make it easy to keep track of these familial connections as you enter them.

Adding a Spouse

The Family Page screen is designed to include information about the husband, wife, and children, and it provides you with data fields in which you can type certain basic facts about each one. Now that you have entered the information about the husband, it is time to add the wife.

1. Type the **wife's name** in the Wife field and **press** the **Tab key**. The cursor will move to the Date born field.

2. Enter the **birth date** in the Date born field and **press** the **Tab key**. The cursor will move to the in field.

3. Type the **place of birth** in the in field and **press** the **Tab key**. The cursor will move to the Died field.

4. Enter the **death date** in the Died field and **press** the **Tab key**. The cursor will move to the in field.

5. Type the **place of death** in the **in** field and **press** the **Tab key**. The cursor will move to the Buried field.

6. Enter the **burial date** in the Buried field and **press** the **Tab key**. The cursor will move to the in field.

7. Type the **place of burial** in the in field and **press** the **Tab key**. The cursor will move to the Marriage date field.

8. Enter the **marriage date** in the Marriage date field and **press** the **Tab key** twice. The cursor will move to the Marriage location field.

TIP

The **Beginning status** drop-down list allows you to select the type of relationship between the two individuals. For most of them you will select the **Married** option. For more on this feature, see Chapter 20, "Working with Dates and Facts."

---

9. Type the **place of marriage** in the Marriage location field.

Adding Children

When you add children in the Family Page, you can enter the basics about each child. You can easily enter each child's full name, gender, and date of birth.

1. Type the **name** of the first child in the 1 field and **press** the **Tab key**. The cursor will move to the Sex field.

2. Enter the **sex** and **press** the **Tab key**. The cursor will move to the Birth dates field.

3. Type the **date of birth** and **press** the **Tab key**. The cursor will move to the name field for the next child.

NOTE

You can add as many children as necessary. When you press the Tab key after each birth date, Family Tree Maker takes you to the next child line, where you can enter the information for the next child. For more on this, see Chapter 4, "Enhancing the Family."

Adding an Additional Spouse

The Family Page screen allows only one spouse to be displayed at a time. However, there are times when a researcher needs to enter more than one spouse for an individual. Family Tree Maker is capable of listing multiple spouses.

1. In the Family Page view, **click** on the **Spouses button**. The Spouses of dialog box will open.

2. Click on the **Create a new spouse button**. A message box will appear, asking if you want the new spouse to be associated with the children previously entered for an individual.

3a. Click on **Yes**. The children will have the new spouse as one of their parents.

OR

3b. Click on **No**. The children will not have the new spouse added as their parent.

4. In the Wife field, **type** the **name** of the new spouse.

5. Enter the **information** you know about the marriage event.

Designating a Preferred Spouse

In reports, as well as in the Family Page window, Family Tree Maker requires that one spouse be selected as the preferred spouse.

1. In the Family Page view, **click** on the **Spouses button**. The Spouses of dialog box will open.

NOTE

Notice that the Spouses button now displays two individuals. This lets you know that the person has more than one spouse.

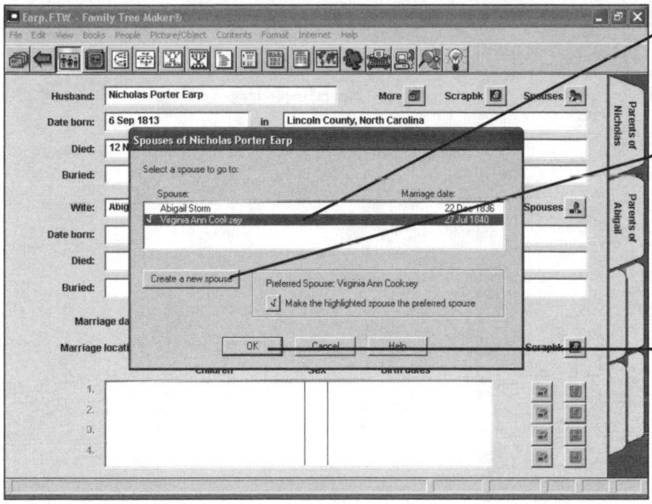

2. Click on the **spouse** you want to appear as the preferred spouse. The spouse will be highlighted.

3. Click on the **Make the highlighted spouse the preferred spouse button.** The preferred spouse character will appear at the left of the selected individual.

4. Click on **OK**. The Spouses of dialog box will close.

Switching to Another Spouse

Because you can only view the information and children of one spouse, it is necessary to switch spouses when you want to work on that specific family. You also need to change spouses if you want to add additional information about that particular marriage.

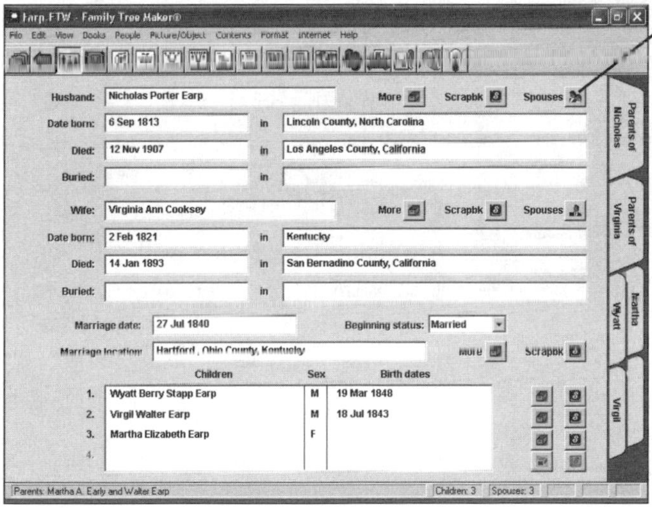

1. Click on the **Spouses button**. The Spouses of dialog box will open.

2. Select the **spouse** for the marriage on which you want to work. The spouse will be highlighted.

3. Click on **OK**. The Spouses of dialog box will close.

NOTE

The Family Page view now displays the selected spouse, even though you have not made this spouse the preferred spouse. You can edit information about the spouse or the marriage or add additional children at this point.

TIP

Family Tree Maker will tell you how many children and spouses are known for the individual highlighted in the Family Page.

Moving a Child to the Primary Individual Position

After you have entered the children, it is possible that you will want to concentrate on a specific child. To do this, you move that child to the primary husband or wife position.

1. Drag the **scroll bar** next to the children information until you find the child with whom you want to work.

NOTE

The names that appear in the tabs at the right of the screen will change as the names in the Children section change.

2. **Click** on the **tab** for the selected child.

The child will replace the parent in the Husband or Wife field, and all of the other fields on the Family Page will change in accordance with the information currently known about that child.

PART II

Using Family Tree Maker Features

Chapter 4
Enhancing the Family 47

Chapter 5
Documenting Sources 63

Chapter 6
Understanding More
About Options 83

Chapter 7
Using More About Notes ..97

Chapter 8
Working with More
About Marriage 115

Chapter 9
Getting into Individual
Facts Cards 123

4 Enhancing the Family

The family structure in a genealogical search is constantly changing. You are always finding new individuals that need to be connected in your database. In this chapter, you'll learn how to:

- Add parents
- Add additional parents
- Add siblings
- Arrange children

Adding Parents

It is likely that when you were working through Chapter 3, "Family Tree Maker for Beginners," you entered information about your immediate family. Now you will want to add the parents of one of those people you entered.

1. Click on the **Family Page button**. The Family Page will appear.

2. Click on the **Parents tab** for either the husband or the wife. The new Family Page window with the basic information for one child will be displayed. The child whose basic information is displayed is the individual who was the husband or wife in the previous screen.

3. Enter the **father's name** in the Husband field.

4. Enter the **father's birth and death information** in the appropriate fields.

NOTE

Family Tree Maker doesn't care about the last name of the parent. The links from parent to child or child to parent are not based on the surname but on how you enter the individuals into the program through the Family Page.

5. Enter the **mother's name** in the Wife field.

6. Enter the **mother's birth and death information** in the appropriate fields.

TIP

When typing the names of females, you will always enter them with their maiden name. That is the surname they had at birth.

NOTE

There will be times when you do not know the maiden name of the woman. The proper way to enter an unknown surname is to use the following set of characters: [--?--]. However, be aware that Family Tree Maker will question such a surname.

7. Type the **parents' marriage date** in the Marriage date field.

8. Select a **beginning status** from the Beginning status drop-down list. You will probably choose Married for this option.

9. Enter a **marriage location** in the Marriage location field.

> **TIP**
>
> If you prefer not to use your mouse, press the Tab key after entering the marriage date. This will take you to the Beginning status drop-down list. You can then change the status by pressing the up or down arrow key. When you have selected the Beginning status you want, press the Tab key to move the cursor to the Marriage location field.

Working with Children

It is in the Family Page that you would add siblings for your previously entered individuals. Additionally, it is through the Children fields that you have the opportunity to add another set of parents in addition to the child's natural, or biological, parents.

Adding Siblings

After you have added the information for the parents, you will want to work on your ancestor's siblings.

1. Click in the **Name field for the next known child**.

2. Type the **name** of the next known child, as well as the rest of the information known about that child.

3. Enter the **next child's information** and continue to **add information** for the rest of the children in the family.

There may be times when the children you have entered are not in their correct birth order. You will learn how to adjust their order in the "Arranging Child Order" section later in this chapter.

Adding Another Set of Parents

In cases of adoption, there will be times when you have two sets of parents for an individual. Or, in other cases, an individual might have a step-parent. Naturally, you want to record all the information for that person.

1. Click on the **child** you wish to select. The child will be selected.

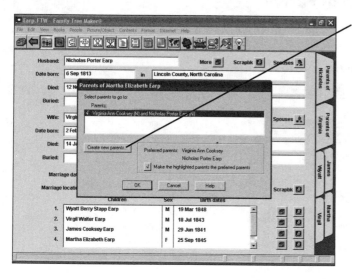

2. Click on **People**. The People menu will appear.

3. Click on **Other Parents**. The Parents of dialog box will open.

4. Click on the **Create new parents button**. The Create New Parents dialog box will open.

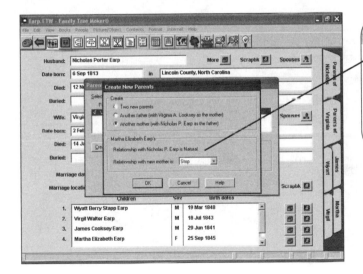

5. Choose between **Two new parents, Another father, or Another mother**.

NOTE

Notice that when you select Another father or Another mother, the relationship options reflect the selection. You can only change the relationship for the chosen parent.

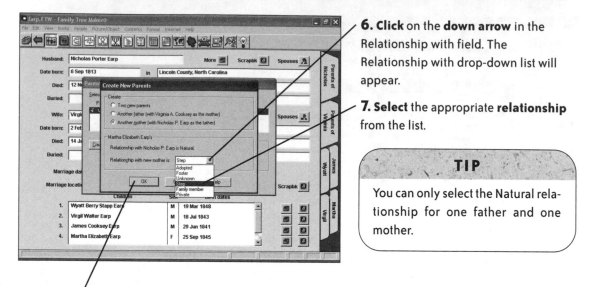

6. **Click** on the **down arrow** in the Relationship with field. The Relationship with drop-down list will appear.

7. **Select** the appropriate **relationship** from the list.

> **TIP**
>
> You can only select the Natural relationship for one father and one mother.

8. **Click** on **OK** to accept the selection. The Create New Parents dialog box will close and a message box will appear, asking you whether the child's siblings should be attached to the new parent(s).

9a. **Click** on **Yes** to attach the siblings to the new parent(s).

OR

9b. **Click** on **No** to attach only the selected child to the new parent(s).

10. Type the **parent's name** in the appropriate name field. Notice that the information for the remaining parent has carried over, and that the child's information has been brought to the new screen.

Arranging Child Order

In a perfect world, you would already know everything about all the children in a particular family. However, this is not usually the case. There will be times when you will need to add a child or change the order of the children previously entered.

Adding a Child

The best way to add an additional child to the list of children is to select the Insert Child option.

1. Click on the **Family Page button**. The Family Page window will open.

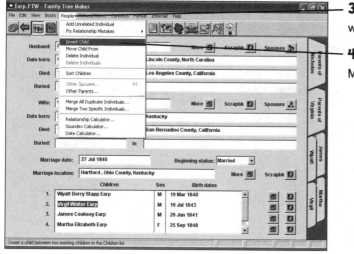

2. In the Children field, **click** on the **row** where you want to insert the new child.

3. Click on **People**. The People menu will appear.

4. Click on **Insert Child**. Family Tree Maker will insert a blank child row.

5. Enter the **name** of the new child and **press** the **Tab key**. The cursor will move to the Sex field.

6. Type the **sex** of the new child and **press** the **Tab key**. The cursor will move to the Birth dates field.

7. Enter the **birth date** of the new child.

Moving a Child

After you have entered or updated a child's information, you might need to move the child so that he or she appears in the proper birth order.

1. Select the **child** you wish to move. The child will be selected.

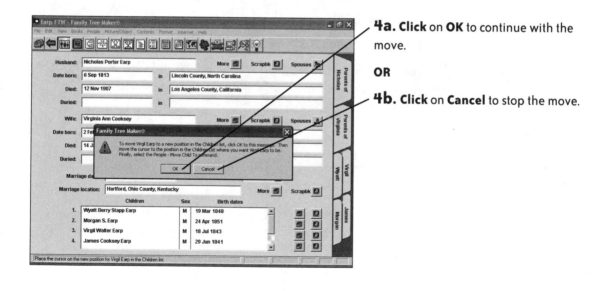

2. Click on **People**. The People menu will appear.

3. Click on **Move Child From**. A message box will appear, telling you how to move the child into a new position in the Children list.

4a. Click on **OK** to continue with the move.

OR

4b. Click on **Cancel** to stop the move.

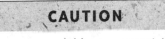

5. In the Children field, **click** on the **position** to which you want to move the child.

6. Click on **People**. The People menu will appear.

7. Click on **Move Child To**. The child will move to the new position.

CAUTION

To move a child, you cannot just type over the previously entered child's name. Family Tree Maker uses internal tracking that is not altered when you do this. If there are spouses or descendants associated with the original child, such a manual change could nullify the links previously created.

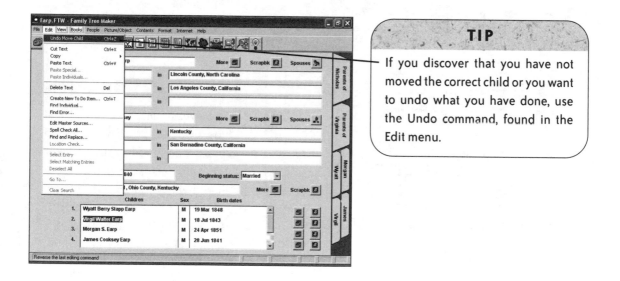

Sorting Children

If you are working with records that do not list the children in order, it is not necessary to figure out the correct order before entering them on the Family Page. Family Tree Maker offers a Sort command that will rearrange the children chronologically after you have entered them.

1. Click on **People**. The People menu will appear.

2. Click on **Sort Children**. A dialog box will appear, confirming that you want to sort the children by birth order (oldest first).

3. Click on **OK** to have Family Tree Maker arrange the children in this order.

5

Documenting Sources

Citing the sources of your family history information is one of the most important aspects of your research. Citing sources helps you keep track of the records you have used, which helps you avoid wasting time revisiting sources. In this chapter, you'll learn how to:

- Determine where you can cite a source
- Cite a source
- Create a master source
- Change a master source
- Search for a master source

Where Can You Cite Sources?

Family Tree Maker makes it possible for you to cite sources for the names of individuals and each of their specific events. This allows you to document your research so that others with whom you share information will know what you used to draw your conclusions.

1. Click on the **Family Page button**. The Family Page will appear.

2. Click on **View**. The View Menu will appear.

3. Click on **Source**. The Source-Citation dialog box will open.

You can cite sources in several fields, including these:

- Name
- Birth date and location
- Death date and location
- Burial date and location
- Marriage date and location
- Marriage ending date and location
- Each of the Custom Fact fields (found in the More About window)
- Cause of death (found in the More About Medical window)
- Medical information (found in the More About Medical window)

Citing a Source

There are a few steps you need to take to create a source and cite it as proof of an individual event (or of a person's life as a whole). You will first create a master source listing, which can be selected from a list the next time you cite that source.

Creating a Master Source

The master source has fields for the source details that don't change. For example, the author, title, and publication information don't change for a book. Items like the page number from which the information comes, however, will change depending on the person about whom you are entering data.

1. Click on **Edit**. The Edit menu will appear.

2. Click on **Edit Master Sources**. The Master Source dialog box will open.

> ### TIP
>
> You only need to enter a source one time. You can then recall it from the list the next time you want to cite it as proof of an individual's specific event. This is especially useful when a lot of information comes from a single source, such as a book. Remember that for every event or conclusion you include in your Family File, you should have a source cited.

3. Type the **book title** in the Title of source field and **press** the **Tab key**. The rest of the fields will be activated and the cursor will move to the Author/Originator field.

> ### NOTE
>
> The Title of source field has been programmed so that the title will print out in italics when source citations are included on reports.

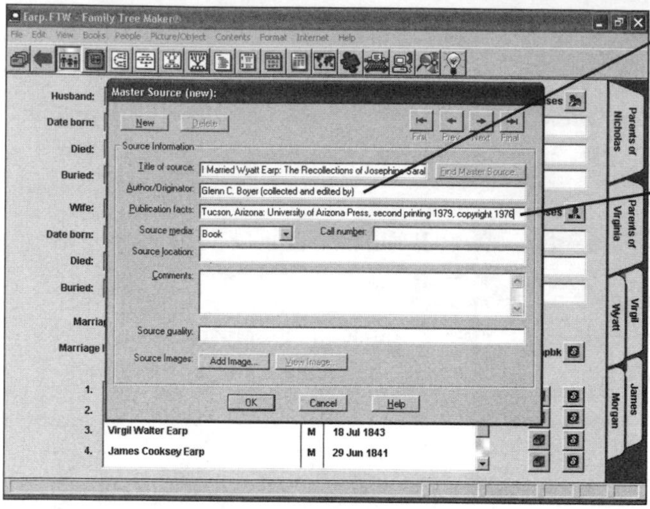

4. Enter the **author's name** in the Author/Originator field and **press** the **Tab key**. The cursor will move to the Publication facts field.

5. Type the **publication information**.

TIP

Publication information includes the place of publication, the name of the publishing company, and the copyright date. The format is Provo, Utah: MyFamily.com, Inc., 2003.

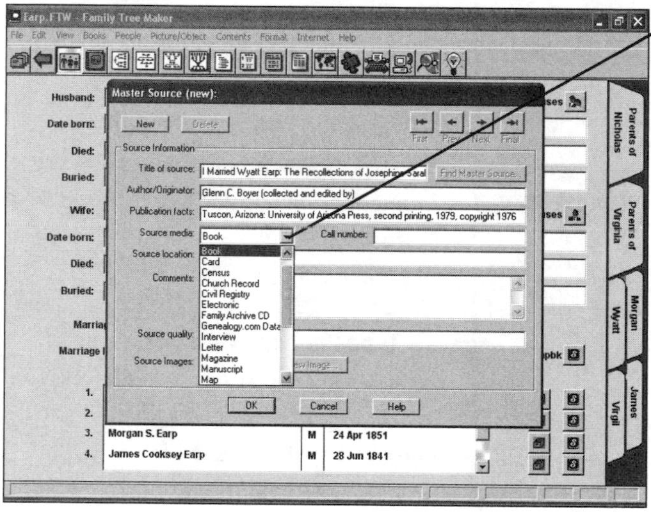

6. Select the **type of media** from the Source media drop-down menu.

NOTE

Including the source media type enables you to quickly see what the original source was. This will help you later when you need to evaluate the proof used in drawing the conclusions you made.

7. Type the **call number** in the Call number field and **press** the **Tab key**. The cursor will move to the Source location field.

NOTE

The call number is the number assigned to the source in the repository where it was found. This could be a microfilm number, a Dewey Decimal system number, or some other numbering system unique to that particular library or archive.

8. Enter the **source location** and **press** the **Tab key**. The cursor will move to the Comments field.

NOTE

The source location might be a library, archive, county courthouse, or cousin's residence. The source location is where the original source used exists. Recording this gives you a place to turn should you need to revisit that original.

9. Type your **comments** and **press** the **Tab key**. The cursor will move to the Source quality field.

NOTE

The Comments section offers you a place to put your thoughts about the source and the information included in that source. This information is not included when the source is printed on reports; it is only for your personal reference.

---

10. Enter the **quality** of the source.

NOTE

The quality of the source is one reference to how reliable the source is. If the source is difficult to read because of unclear handwriting or faded ink, then it is possible that the information found could be questioned.

11. Click on **OK**. The Master Source dialog box will close.

Using the Source-Citation Dialog Box

The Source-Citation dialog box is where you will select the appropriate master source for the information you are citing. You can enter source information when you enter the data and details for each ancestor.

1. Click in the **field** where you want to add a source citation.

2. Click on **View**. The View menu will appear.

3. Click on **Source**. The Source-Citation dialog box will open.

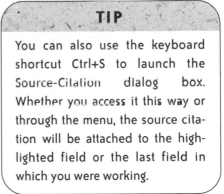

TIP

You can also use the keyboard shortcut Ctrl+S to launch the Source-Citation dialog box. Whether you access it this way or through the menu, the source citation will be attached to the highlighted field or the last field in which you were working.

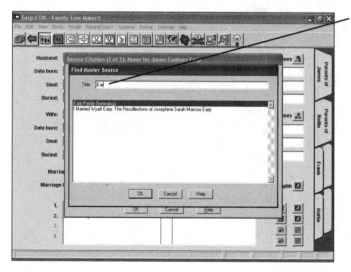

4. Click on the **Find Master Source button**. The Find Master Source dialog box will open.

5. Type part of the **title** in the Title field. Family Tree Maker will highlight the first title that matches the word you've typed.

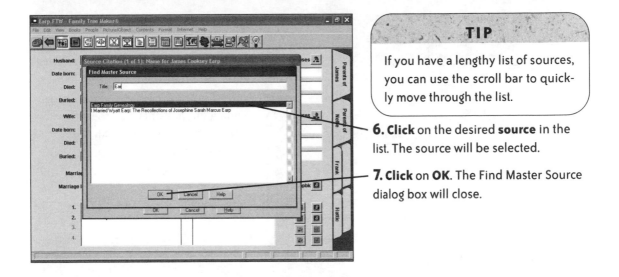

If you have a lengthy list of sources, you can use the scroll bar to quickly move through the list.

6. Click on the desired **source** in the list. The source will be selected.

7. Click on **OK**. The Find Master Source dialog box will close.

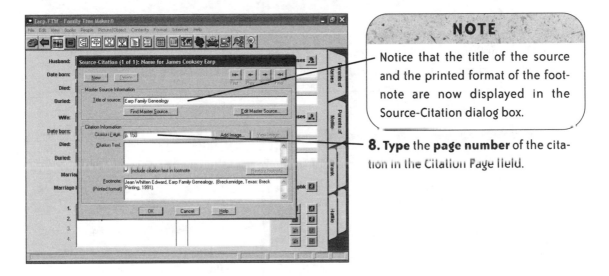

Notice that the title of the source and the printed format of the footnote are now displayed in the Source-Citation dialog box.

8. Type the **page number** of the citation in the Citation Page field.

Not all source citations will have a page number included on this screen. For more information about source citations, read Elizabeth Shown Mills's *Evidence! Citation and Analysis for the Family Historian* (Genealogical Publishing Co., 1997).

9. Enter the **Citation text** in the Citation Text field. The citation text might be additional identifying information. For instance, when citing a census record, you would want to include the Enumeration District, Supervisor's District, Dwelling number, and Family number for the specific house of your ancestor on that census page.

TIP

You can decide whether to include text from the Citation Text field in the printed footnote. Click on the Include citation text in footnote check box if you want the text to be included. If the text is just for your information, make sure the box is not checked.

10. Click on **OK** to close the Source-Citation dialog box.

NOTE

Notice that there is now an "s" next to the field where you elected to cite the source. This is how you know that you have cited a source for either an individual or an event.

Creating a Master Source from the Source-Citation Dialog Box

Few of us are so organized that we already know all of the sources that we will be citing before we begin. While you're working on a family, you might find that an obscure source was not added to the master source list earlier. You do not need to exit out of the Source-Citation dialog box to add a master source.

1. Press Ctrl+S to open the Source-Citation dialog box.

NOTE

It is possible that the Source-Citation dialog box already has a previously cited source. You can have more than one source citation per person or event.

2. Click on the **New button**. Family Tree Maker will start a new source citation, and the cursor will move to the Title of source field.

3. Type the **title** of the new source. The Edit Master Source button will be activated.

4. Click on the **Edit Master Source button**. The Master Source dialog box will open.

TIP

Notice that the Title of source field has been disabled in the Master Source dialog box. You cannot change the title at this time. For more information on editing master sources, see the "Changing a Master Source" section later in this chapter.

5. Enter the **appropriate source information**.

6. Click on **OK**. The Master Source dialog box will close.

You can now complete the source citation with the page number and citation text as you learned in the "Using the Source-Citation Dialog Box" section earlier in this chapter.

7. Click on **OK**. The Source-Citation dialog box will close.

Changing a Master Source

While we would all like to think we are perfect, there will be times when you will discover that you've made an error. In a source, that should be fixed as soon as it is noticed. Usually you will notice such an error when you're working with that source in the Source-Citation dialog box.

1. Click on **View**. The View menu will appear.

2. Click on **Source**. The Source-Citation dialog box will open.

3. Click on the **Find Master Source button**. The Find Master Source dialog box will open.

4. Select a **master source** from the list of available sources.

5. Click on **OK**. The Find Master Source dialog box will close. You will notice that the Edit Master Source button has now been activated in the Source-Citation dialog box.

6. Click on the **Edit Master Source button**. The Master Source dialog box will open.

7. Make the appropriate **changes** to the master source fields. Usually you'll be changing a typo or fixing the publication date.

> **NOTE**
>
> The Title of source field is grayed out when you access the master source in this manner. To edit the title of a master source, see "Editing a Master Source" in the next section.

8. Click on **OK**. The Master Source dialog box will close.

> **NOTE**
>
> Notice that the changes you made to the source have taken effect in the printed format of the footnote.

Editing a Master Source

While accessing the master source through the Source-Citation dialog box is easy, you cannot change the title of the source this way. If you have a lot of editing to do to a master source, you might want to go directly to the master source.

1. Click on **Edit**. The Edit menu will appear.

2. Click on Edit Master Sources. The Master Source dialog box will open.

TIP

You can use the Next, Prev, First, and Final buttons to skip through previously entered master sources. Click on the New button to create a new master source, and use the Delete button to delete the currently displayed master source.

If you inadvertently type over the name of a source in the Source-Citation dialog box, Family Tree Maker will ask you whether you want to change the present title or create a new source.

Searching for a Master Source

There will be times when you will want to look at a specific master source. The easiest way to do this is through the Master Source dialog box.

1. Click on **Edit**. The Edit menu will appear.

2. Click on **Edit Master Sources.** The Master Source dialog box will open.

3. Click on the **Find Master Source button**. The Find Master Source dialog box will open.

NOTE

You then would type in the first few letters of the source in question as you did earlier in this chapter when working in "Using the Source-Citation Dialog Box."

Attaching Images to Sources

Modern technology affords us the ability to scan documents or microfilm to digitize documents. Family Tree Maker offers you the capability to attach such an image to the Master Source or the specific Source-Citation dialog box.

1. Press Ctrl + S. The Source-Citation dialog box will open.

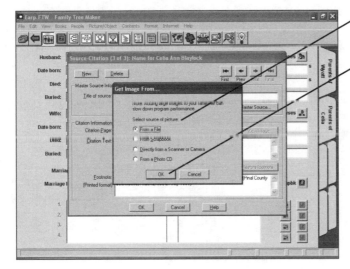

2. Click on the **Add Image button**. The Get Image From dialog box will open.

3. Select the appropriate **source** of the picture. The option will be selected.

4. Click on **OK**. Family Tree Maker will open a window or launch the appropriate program.

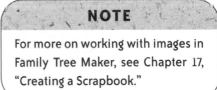

NOTE

For more on working with images in Family Tree Maker, see Chapter 17, "Creating a Scrapbook."

6

Understanding More About Options

Family history is much more than just names and dates of birth or death. As you research further into your family's generations, you will be keeping track of additional events and wanting to add family stories. In this chapter, you'll learn how to:

- Add and work with additional facts
- Add addresses for living relatives
- Track medical information
- Work with the More About Lineage window

Working with the More About Facts Window

Family Tree Maker offers you a way to track additional life events. As your research progresses, you will find that you are relying on such things as probate records and church records, in addition to the more recognizable vital records. Family Tree Maker has included a variety of predefined facts (Family Tree Maker's name for the events in a person's life) to help you record this information.

1. Click on the **Family Page button**. The Family Page will appear.

2. Click on the **More button**. The More About window will appear.

3. Click on the **Facts button**. The More About Facts window will appear.

NOTE

You can also access the More About options from the View menu.

Adding Custom Facts

You will record much of the information about your ancestors in the More About Facts window. This is where you will record the variety of life events that you discover.

1. Click on the **Fact down arrow**. The Fact drop-down menu will appear.

2. Click on a **fact** in the menu. The fact will be selected and the menu will close.

3. Press the **Tab key** to advance to the Date field.

> ### TIP
>
> Many of the facts in the Fact drop-down menu are pertinent to specific religions. This allows you to select the appropriate religious event, rather than making do with, say, a general christening event.

4. Type the **date** of the event and **press** the **Tab key**. The cursor will move to the Comment/Location field.

> ### TIP
>
> Information entered using the More About options can also be added using the Individual Facts Card. For more on this option, see Chapter 9, "Getting into Individual Facts Cards."

5. Enter the **event location** and **press** the **Tab key**. The new fact will be added, in chronological order, to the list of facts for that individual, for those events with full dates.

NOTE

The Pref'd check box is disabled for event-type facts, unless you have conflicting or duplicated facts. If you had two death dates, you would select one of them as your preferred choice.

Adding Additional Names

There are times when you will discover that your ancestor had another name. It might have been a religious name or a nickname, or it might just be a variant of his or her given name. Family Tree Maker allows you to keep track of these different names. Whereas the AKA (also known as) name option allows you to record one additional name, through the name options here you can record variant name spellings and other names you simply want to remember.

1. Click on the **Fact down arrow**. The Fact drop-down menu will appear.

2. Select the **Name fact** and **press** the **Tab key**. The cursor will move to the Comment/Location field.

3. Enter the **individual's alternate name**.

4a. Click on the **Pref'd check box** if you want this name to be the one used in the Family Page and on reports.

OR

4b. Leave the **Pref'd check box** empty if you do not want this name used in the Family Page and on reports.

TIP

Click on the Pref'd check box next to the name you wish to use as the preferred name. This will put the preferred name at the top of the list of names and tells Family Tree Maker which name you want used when generating reports.

Creating a New Fact Name

Family Tree Maker includes forty-one different facts, but you might need to record an event that is not covered by any of them. You can create a new fact name whenever you need one.

1. Click in the **Fact field**.

2. Type the **name** of the new event and **press** the **Tab key**. The cursor will move to the Date field.

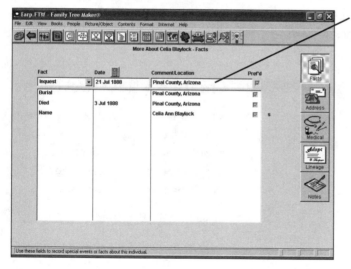

3. Enter the **date** and **press** the **Tab key**. The cursor will move to the Comment/Location field.

> **NOTE**
>
> You can use partial dates, or estimate the date based on the individuals age at another time. To estimate dates, see "Calculating Dates and Ages" in Chapter 20 "Working with Dates and Facts."

4. Type the **event location** and **press** the **Tab key**. Family Tree Maker will open a New Fact Name message box, verifying that you want to accept the new fact name.

5a. Click on **OK** to accept the new fact name. The new fact name will be saved.

OR

5b. Click on **Cancel** to return to the Fact field to type in a different name or select a different predefined fact.

NOTE

You can always get rid of a fact name that you have created. For more information on this, see Chapter 20, "Working with Dates and Facts."

Using the Address Window

The Address window is useful when you're entering data about your living relatives. People involved with a family association rely heavily on this for mailing lists, as do those who want to keep track of family members with whom they are exchanging information.

1. Click on the **Address button**. The More About Address and Phone(s) window will appear.

NOTE

Notice that the individual's name has already been supplied. Family Tree Maker assumes you are entering the address for the individual currently in the More About window.

2. Type the **street address** in the Street 1 field and **press** the **Tab key** twice. The cursor will move to the City field.

3. Type the **city name** and **press** the **Tab key**. The cursor will move to the State or province field.

4. Type the **state or province** and **press** the **Tab key**. The cursor will move to the Zip or postal code field.

5. Enter the **zip or postal code** and **press** the **Tab key**. The cursor will move to the Country field.

6. Type the **country name** and **press** the **Tab key**. The cursor will move to the Phone(s) field.

7. Enter the **phone number** and **press** the **Tab key**. The cursor will move to the E-mail(s) field.

8. Enter the **e-mail address**.

NOTE

The More About Address is also a great place to record the address of your deceased ancestors as found in a particular city directory.

Working with Medical Information

Modern medical technology has made understanding your medical family tree more obviously important than ever before. Family Tree Maker provides you with space for recording pertinent medical information about your family members and ancestors.

1. Click on the **Medical button**. The More About Medical window will appear.

2. Type the **height** in feet and inches in the Height field and **press** the **Tab key**. The cursor will move to the Weight field.

3. Enter the **weight** in pounds and ounces in the Weight field and **press** the **Tab key**. The cursor will move to the Cause of death field.

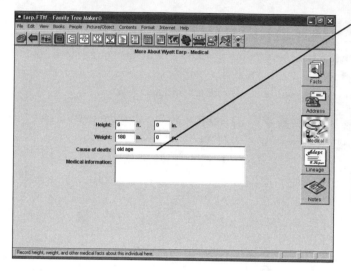

4. **Type** the **cause of death** and **press** the **Tab key**. The cursor will move to the Medical information field.

> **NOTE**
>
> The cause of death will generally be the medical term found on the death certificate, or the illness or condition that caused the individual to die.

5. In the Medical information field, **enter** the **details** you feel are important about your ancestor's medical history.

> **NOTE**
>
> The Medical information field can hold up to 200 characters of information, which is about five lines of text.

Opening the More About Lineage Window

Family Tree Maker uses the More About Lineage window to organize information about relationships, titles, and aliases.

1. Click on the **Lineage button**. The More About Lineage window will appear.

2. Enter any appropriate **information** or **select** one of the available **options**. The following sections will describe some of the different options available in this window.

TIP

When entering a title, do not enter items such as Jr. or III. The titles entered here will be printed in front of the individual's name on reports. If your ancestor was a Jr. or a Sr., this is typed into the Name field on the Family Page, at the end of the name and following a comma. When you are indexing your book, the comma becomes necessary in order to distinguish Jr. from the surname. Family Tree Maker automatically recognizes roman numerals such as III or IV, so no comma is necessary.

Entering AKA Names

You will, perhaps, discover a name change or an alternate name for an ancestor or family member. Legal name changes are just one way the AKA field can be used.

1. Click in the **This person is also known as (aka) field** and **type** the **also known as name** for your ancestor.

TIP

When you print reports, you can elect to use the also known as name instead of or in addition to the name used in the Family Page view. Such decisions are made when you are working in the individual report. For more on this topic, see Chapter 16, "Creating Genealogy Style and Genealogical Source Reports."

Working with Special Relationships

As you dig deeper into your family history, you are apt to discover mothers who died early, fathers who remarried, adoptions, and other unique relationship situations. It is easy to record these in Family Tree Maker.

NOTE

You will want to pay attention to the names in the Relationship section. How these individuals will be connected to each other will be affected as you make changes in the Relationship section.

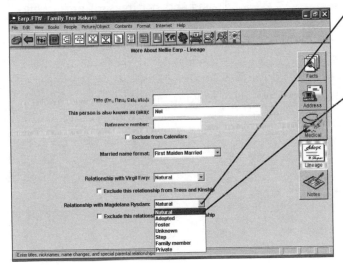

1. Click on the **Relationship with down arrow** next to the father's name. The Relationship drop-down menu will appear.

2. Select the appropriate **relationship** between the father and the individual.

> ## NOTE
>
> You will only be able to select Natural from the drop-down menu for one father and one mother, regardless of how many parents you have added to a person.

3. Click on the **Relationship with down arrow** next to the mother's name. The Relationship drop-down menu will appear.

4. Select the appropriate **relationship** between the mother and the individual.

Excluding Relationships

At times you might want to exclude information from reports you send to family members, possibly out of respect for their feelings. Some of those exclusions are set up in the More About Lineage window.

1. Click on the **Exclude this relationship from Trees and Kinship check box** for either the mother or the father of the individual. The option will be selected and that relationship will be excluded from your reports.

NOTE

Electing to exclude the relationship from Trees and Kinship can dramatically affect reports. Kinship reports and Ancestor Trees will exclude the paternal and/or maternal ancestors, depending on which relationship(s) you chose to exclude. Descendant trees will exclude the child and the child's descendants.

7

Using More About Notes

One way to make your family history interesting to other family members is to include family stories. With Family Tree Maker you can do just that. In this chapter, you'll learn how to:

- Enter notes and stories
- Copy and move notes and stories
- Find text in notes
- Import notes
- Export notes
- Format notes for printing

Working with Notes and Stories

Most of us have heard our grandparents, aunts, or uncles share stories about family members. As your research progresses, you will find additional stories that you will want to preserve for future generations. Family Tree Maker's More About Notes section allows you to easily incorporate these notes and stories into your research.

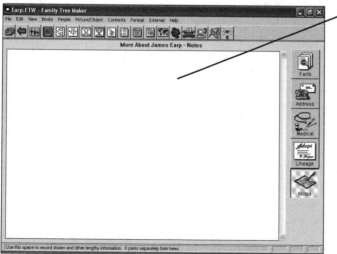

Entering Notes and Stories

The More About Notes window allows you to enter, in a narrative style, the stories or research notes you want to include in your reports.

1. Click on **View**. The View menu will appear.

2. Move the **mouse pointer** to More About. The More About menu will appear.

3. Click on **Notes**. The More About Notes window will appear.

4. In the text box, **enter** the **text** you wish to include for the individual.

NOTE

The information typed into the Notes window will not print on the family tree styled reports. However, you can print this information on a family group sheet report or include it in a book.

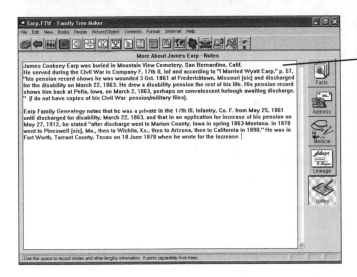

TIP

When quoting information from a source, be sure to include the source citation information. Always put quotation marks around any information that is a direct quote from a published source.

Copying Notes and Stories

Sometimes a particular note might apply to more than one individual. When you are working with such a story, you will want to take advantage of the copy and paste functions available in Family Tree Maker.

1. Click on **View**. The View menu will appear.

2. Click on **Individual Facts Card**. The Individual Facts Card will appear.

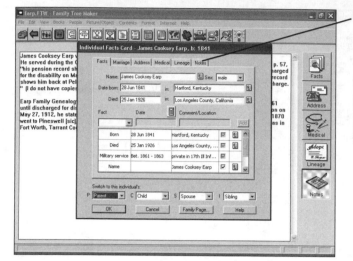

3. Click on **Notes**. The Notes tab will appear.

> **TIP**
>
> This is another method of getting to the Notes window for a particular individual.

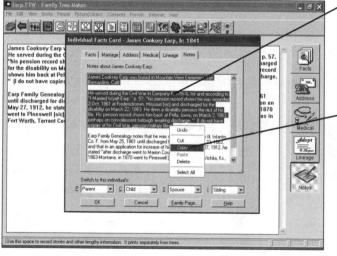

4. Click and drag the **mouse pointer** to highlight the desired text. The text will be selected.

5. Right-click on the selected **text**. The right mouse menu will appear.

6. Click on **Copy**. The selected text will be placed on the Clipboard, ready for you to paste wherever you like. Chapter 10, "Searching Your Family Tree File," explains how to locate someone in your database who is not included in the current Family Page window. You can use these functions to locate an individual to whose Notes window you want to paste the copied text.

> **TIP**
>
> The menu that appears when you right-click is a shortcut menu that allows you to cut, copy, paste, or delete selected text. This is similar to clicking on the Edit menu and selecting the options there.

Moving Notes and Stories

You might discover that a story you thought pertained to one individual was really about another. The easiest way to fix this is to move the story from one More About Notes window to another.

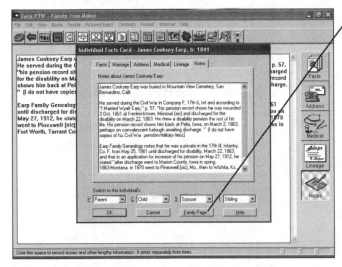

1. Click on the **Family Page button** on the Individual Facts Card. The Family Page will appear.

2. Click on the **More button**. The More About window will appear.

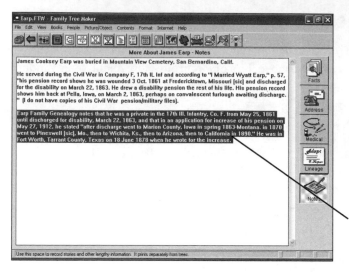

NOTE

If you were last working in a More About Notes view, then the More About Notes window will be displayed when you click the More button for another person. If you weren't working in a More About Notes window earlier, then you will need to click on the Notes button.

3. Click and drag the **mouse pointer** to highlight the text in question.

4. Click on **Edit**. The Edit menu will appear.

5. Click on **Cut Text**. The selected text will be removed from the More About Notes window and placed on the Clipboard, ready to be pasted in another individual's More About Notes window.

6. Click on the **Family Page button**. The Family Page window will appear.

7. Click on the **Name tab** of the individual you want to select. The Family Page window will change to reflect the selected individual.

8. Click on the **More button**. The More About Notes window should be displayed because it was the last More About window used.

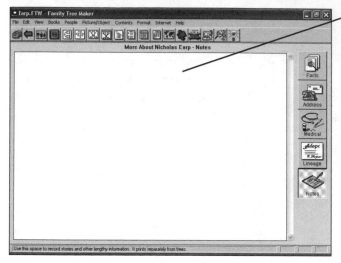

9. Click inside the **text box**.

10. Click on **Edit**. The Edit menu will appear.

11. Click on **Paste Text**. The text will appear in the More About Notes window.

> **TIP**
>
> The keyboard shortcuts Ctrl+X for Cut, Ctrl+C for Copy, and Ctrl+V for Paste can be used instead of the menus.

Finding Text in Notes

It can be hard to find one particular sentence or thought when you have typed a large amount of text in the More About Notes window. Family Tree Maker offers a way to search for a specific word or phrase. Before you follow these directions, be sure the More About Notes window you want to search is open.

1. Click on **Edit**. The Edit menu will appear.

2. Click on **Find**. The Find dialog box will open.

3. Type the **word or phrase** for which you want to search in the Find what field.

4. Click on the **Find next button**. When Family Tree Maker finds the requested word or phrase, it will highlight it in the More About Notes window.

TIP

Family Tree Maker allows you to match whole words or match case. This allows you to eliminate those words that share consecutive letters with the word for which you are looking.

NOTE

If the cursor was not at the beginning of the text in the More About Notes window, then Family Tree Maker might ask you if you want to continue searching from the beginning. Click on **Yes** if you want to continue searching.

5. Click on the **Find next button** to continue searching the text.

6. Click on **OK** when you see the message box telling you that Family Tree Maker has reached the end of the text. The message box will close and you will be returned to the Find dialog box.

7. Click on **Cancel**. The Find dialog box will close.

Importing Text to Notes

At some point, you might want to import some text into Family Tree Maker. You might have received a write-up via e-mail, or you might have already typed up a family story that you now want to place in the More About Notes window. You can do so by importing the text or by copying and pasting.

Copying Text

The Windows operating system allows you to copy text from one application and paste it into another. Because Family Tree Maker is a Windows program, this option is available to you.

1. Highlight the **text** you want to copy from the e-mail message or word-processing file.

2. Press Ctrl+C to copy the text. The text will be placed on the Clipboard.

3. Click on **Family Tree Maker** in the Windows Taskbar. Family Tree Maker will be maximized.

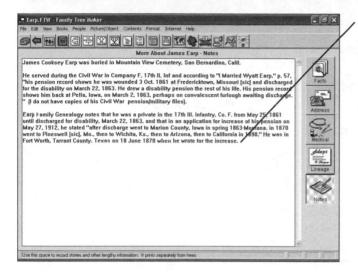

4. Click in the **More About Notes** window, at the location where you want the text to appear. The cursor will appear.

5. Press Ctrl+V. The copied text will appear in the More About Notes window.

Importing Text

Family Tree Maker also allows you to import text. This can be done only when the file you want to import ends in a .txt extension. You need to have the cursor in the More About Notes window where you want the text to appear before you follow these steps.

1. Click on **File**. The File menu will appear.

2. Click on **Import Text File**. The Import Text File dialog box will open.

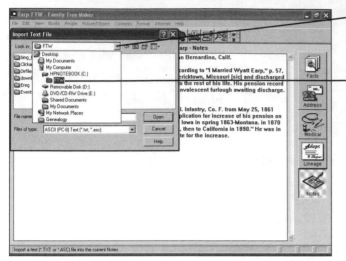

3. Click on the **Look in down arrow**. The Look in drop-down menu will appear.

4. Navigate to the **folder** where the text file is located

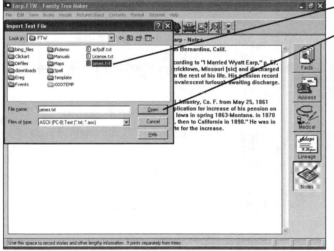

5. Click on the **selected file**.

6. Click on **Open**. The text will be placed in the More About Notes window.

Exporting Notes

You might have notes that you have received from others, and in turn, you might want to share your notes with a cousin or fellow researcher. You can do so by exporting the notes.

1. Click on **File**. The File menu will appear.

2. Move the **mouse pointer** to **Export Notes**. The Export Notes submenu will appear.

3a. Click on **To Acrobat (PDF)**. The Export dialog box will open.

OR

3b. Click on **To Plain Text (TXT)**. The Export dialog box will open.

4. In the File name field, **type** the **name** of the file you want to export. You will want to pay attention to where the file is being saved so you can retrieve it later.

5. Click on **Save**. The text in the More About Notes window will be saved to the file.

TIP

You can also use the copy and paste functions to place the desired text into another application or document.

NOTE

If you selected the PDF export option, Family Tree Maker will open a message box advising you that to read the file you need to have the Adobe Acrobat reader. This is a free reader available at Adobe's website <http://www.adobe.com/>.

Formatting Notes for Printing

With the More About Notes window open, you can format the text's chosen font, style, and size to alter how it appears when printed in the reports. This will make the notes stand out in your report.

1. Click on **Format**. The Format menu will appear.

2. Click on **Text Font, Style, & Size**. A message box will appear, reminding you that the changes made will display only when you print the report, not on the screen.

3. Click on **OK**. The message box will close and the Text Font, Style, & Size dialog box will open.

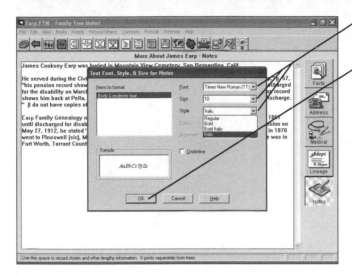

4. Select the desired **font**, **size**, and **style** from the drop-down menus.

5. Click on **OK**. The Text Font, Style, & Size dialog box will close.

> ## NOTE
>
> These formatting options, which are also used in the reports, are discussed in more detail in Chapter 15, "Viewing and Printing Reports and Trees."

> ## TIP
>
> Formatting in the More About Notes window affects all the text in the Notes window, as seen here in this PDF export. You cannot highlight a single paragraph and change the style on just that single paragraph unless the notes are being used in a book. See Chapter 23 "Enhancing Your Family History Book" for more on this.

8

Working with More About Marriage

Much of what you have learned up to this point dealt with a specific individual in your database. However, the marriage event is unique, and Family Tree Maker accommodates the different ways to record it in your database. In this chapter, you'll learn how to:

- Select an ending status for the marriage
- Work with reference numbers
- Select the appropriate marriage fact
- Select a preferred date
- Work with the Marriage Notes window

Accessing the More About Marriage Window

The More About Marriage window allows you to include notes or pertinent additional dates about the marriage of two individuals. While the marriage date itself can be entered on the Family Page, the additional notes and details are entered in the More About Marriage window.

1. Click on the **Family Page button**. The Family Page window will appear.

2. Click on the **Marriage More button**. The More About Marriage window will appear.

3. Click on the **Facts button**. The More About Marriage Facts window will appear.

Using the More About Marriage Facts Window

The More About Marriage Facts window is where you can include additional details about a marriage. This is where you would include a divorce fact or a conflicting marriage fact.

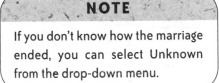

1. Click on the **Ending status down arrow**. The Ending status drop-down menu will appear.

2. Select the appropriate **Ending status** from the menu.

> **NOTE**
>
> If you don't know how the marriage ended, you can select Unknown from the drop-down menu.

Entering a Reference Number

The Reference number field allows you to enter any numbers or letters you choose. If you have a unique filing or pedigree system, you might use this field for that system's reference number.

1a. Type a **reference number** in the Reference number field.

OR

1b. Leave this **field** blank if you do not have a reference numbering system.

> **NOTE**
>
> The Reference number field can hold up to 11 lowercase letters or numbers or combination thereof. The same is true of the Reference number field found in the More About Lineage window, discussed in Chapter 6 "Understanding More About Options."

Adding a Marriage Fact

Although you have already entered one marriage fact, there are others that you might need to enter—possibly a conflicting marriage date or a fact that details the end of that marriage.

1. Click on the **Fact down arrow**. The Fact drop-down menu will appear.

2. Click on the **appropriate fact** from the menu and **press** the **Tab key**. The fact will be selected and the cursor will move to the Date field.

> **TIP**
>
> If you select something like the annulment, divorce, or death of one spouse, be sure to change the Ending status to correspond with the fact.

3. Enter the **date** of the event in the Date field and **press** the **Tab key**. The cursor will move to the Comment/Location field.

4. Type the **location** of the event.

> **TIP**
>
> The small trashcan that shows up when you type a previously-entered place allows you to "trash" what Family Tree Maker is suggesting. If the place is the one you want, you can press the Tab key to accept it and add the fact to the Facts list.

Using the Pref'd Check Box

The Pref'd check box is activated when you have selected a duplicate fact. If, in your research, you discover that you have two conflicting dates, it is a good idea to record both of them. Family Tree Maker then requires you to select one of them as the preferred date for use in the trees and reports.

1. Select a **duplicate fact** from the Fact drop-down menu.

2. Type the **date** of the event in the Date field and **press** the **Tab key**. The cursor will move to the Comment/Location field.

3. Type the **location** of the event and **press** the **Tab key**. The new fact will appear in the Fact list.

NOTE

Notice that at this point the Pref'd check box was already selected for the first marriage entry. The newly added fact does not become the preferred fact. This means it will not be the marriage fact that appears in any reports that you print.

4. Click on the **Pref'd check box** for the second duplicated fact. The newly selected preferred fact will move to the top of the duplicated events and will have a check in the Pref'd check box.

Working with Marriage Notes

Just as you might include stories about an individual as a note, you might also want to record something about a marriage. As it does for individuals, Family Tree Maker supplies you with a More About Notes window for marriages.

1. Click on the **Notes button**. The More About Marriage Notes window will appear.

2. Type the **text** you want to include about the marriage.

NOTE

See Chapter 7, "Using More About Notes," to refresh your memory about changing the text in the More About Notes window.

9 Getting into Individual Facts Cards

With the More About button on the Family Page, you have the ability to enter a lot of different information about a person. Sometimes you want easy access to that information. The Individual Facts Card gives you instant access. In this chapter, you'll learn how to:

- Access the Individual Facts Card

- Establish the Individual Facts Card as a default for editing information

- Add a fact

- Add a note

- Switch to another related individual within the Individual Facts Card

- Add a new related individual to the Family File

- Go to the Family Page

Accessing the Individual Facts Card

The Individual Facts Card was designed to offer you instant access to the information and facts for an individual. You can access this card either through a menu option or through one of the reports.

Opening an Individual Facts Card

Regardless of the view you are using in Family Tree Maker, you can always get to the Individual Facts Card for the primary individual by using the menu option.

1. Click on **View**. The View menu will appear.

2. Click on **Individual Facts Card**. The Individual Facts Card window will appear.

NOTE

If you are in the Family Page view, the View menu is the only way to open the Individual Facts Card.

Accessing the Individual Facts Card from Another View

While you are working in one of the Report views, you might notice that a fact isn't right or that you have a typo in a note. Using the Individual Facts Card, you can immediately correct the problem and then return to the Report view.

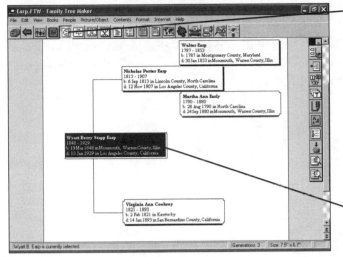

1. Click on a **report button**. The chosen Report view will appear.

NOTE

It may be necessary to select the type of report from a drop-down menu after you have clicked on the Report button of your choice.

2. Double-click on the desired **individual**. The Individual Facts Card for that person will open.

Individual Facts Card Versus the Family Page

Family Tree Maker allows you to choose between the Individual Facts Card or the Family Page when working in other views. In other words, when you double-click on a person in a Report view, you can either be taken to that person's Individual Facts Card or to the Family Page for that person.

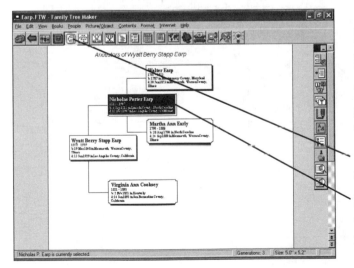

Determining Your Preference

You must first decide which you would prefer to open when working in other views.

1. Click on a **report button**. The chosen Report view will appear.

2. Double-click on the desired **individual**. The Individual Facts Card for that person will open.

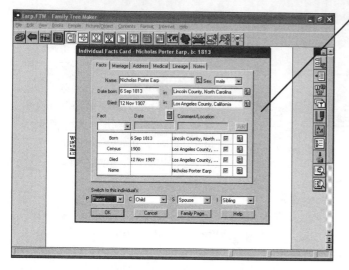

When you have the Individual Facts Card selected as your default, you can make any changes to the individual and then click on OK to return to the Report view.

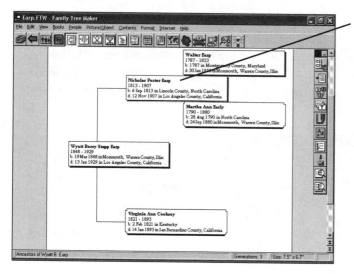

When you access the Family Page from a Report view, it is similar to clicking on the Family Page button in the toolbar. The Family Page view replaces the Report view, and you can work in the More About window or Family Page from there.

TIP

If you have opened the Family Page view from the report, you can return to the Report view by clicking on the Go Back button.

Establishing Your Preference in Family Tree Maker

Once you have experimented with accessing both the Individual Facts Card and the Family Page view from any Report view, you will want to tell Family Tree Maker which you prefer as your default choice when double-clicking on an individual.

1. Click on **File**. The File menu will appear.

2. Click on **Preferences**. The Preferences dialog box will open.

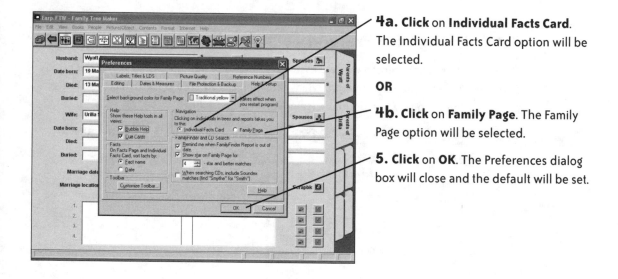

3. Click on the **Help & Setup** tab. The Help & Setup options will be available.

4a. Click on **Individual Facts Card**. The Individual Facts Card option will be selected.

OR

4b. Click on **Family Page**. The Family Page option will be selected.

5. Click on **OK**. The Preferences dialog box will close and the default will be set.

Working with the Individual Facts Card

The Individual Facts Card dialog box offers you instant access to everything currently known about a given individual. You also have the ability to change or add information, and to select or add another related individual.

Adding a Fact

Through the Individual Facts Card, you have the ability to add just as many facts as you do using the More About window.

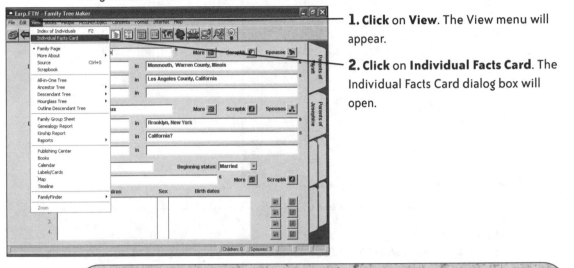

1. Click on **View**. The View menu will appear.

2. Click on **Individual Facts Card**. The Individual Facts Card dialog box will open.

NOTE

If you do not see the Fact, Date, and Comment Location fields above the list of facts for the given individual, you might need to change the display settings in Windows. When Large Fonts has been selected in the display settings, it sometimes forces the list of facts to sit on top of these three fields, which makes it look like they do not work or exist.

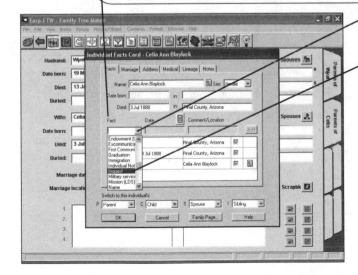

3. Click on the **Fact down arrow**. The Fact drop-down menu will appear.

4. Click on the **appropriate fact**. The fact will be selected and the list will disappear.

5. Press the **Tab key**. The cursor will move to the Date field.

6. Type the **date** and **press** the **Tab key**. The cursor will move to the Comment/Location field.

7. Type the **event location**.

8. Click on the **Add button**. The new fact will be added to the individual's list of facts.

TIP

Just like in the More About Facts window (see Chapter 7, "Using More About Options"), you can create new facts in the Individual Facts Card. Simply type the name of the new fact and press the Tab key. You can then follow steps 6 through 8 above.

Adding a Note

The tabs of the Individual Facts Card mirror the options found in the More About window, accessed from the Family Page. As such, anything that you can add in the More About windows can be added in the Individual Facts Card.

1. Click on the **Notes tab**. The tab will move to the front.

2. Type the **note**.

> ## NOTE
>
> You can access any of the other options, such as the Marriage, Address, or Medical sections, by clicking on the appropriate tab. This brings that section of the Individual Facts Card to the front so that you can work with it. All of these sections mirror their More About equivalents.

Switching to Another Related Individual

While the main menu items are disabled when the Individual Facts Card is open, this does not mean you cannot move to other related individuals. You can change the focus of the Individual Facts card by using the drop-down menus at the bottom of the card.

1. Click on one of the **down arrow choices**. The list of appropriate individuals will appear.

2. Click on the desired **individual**.

The individual will be selected and the Individual Facts Card will pertain to the newly selected individual.

Adding a New Related Individual

Often, as you are entering information about an ancestor, you will find that the record or book that has supplied you with that information will also supply you with the name or details of a previously unknown, related individual. You can add this person using the Individual Facts Card.

1. Click on the appropriate **down arrow**. The corresponding list will appear.

2. Click on the **Add a... menu option**. The menu will disappear and the Individual Facts Card will be blank.

3. Type in the **details** for the new person.

Closing the Individual Facts Card

When you are finished making changes or additions to the individual's card, you can close it. Depending on your choice, you will either be returned to the Report view or taken to the Family Page view.

1a. Click on **OK**. The Individual Facts Card will close and you will be returned to the report view if you opened the Individual Facts card from the report.

OR

1b. Click on the **Family Page button**. The Individual Facts Card will close and you will be taken to the Family Page view for that individual.

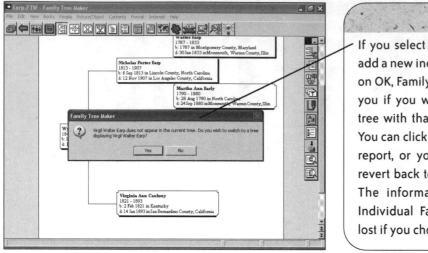

If you select another individual or add a new individual and then click on OK, Family Tree Maker might ask you if you want to pull up a new tree with that individual included. You can click on Yes to redesign the report, or you can click on No to revert back to your original report. The information entered in the Individual Facts Card will not be lost if you choose No.

PART

III

Working in Family Tree Maker

Chapter 10
Searching Your Family Tree File 137

Chapter 11
Correcting Information in Family Tree Maker 157

Chapter 12
Fixing Relationships & Duplicates 173

10

Searching Your Family Tree File

When you first begin entering data, it is easy to use the tabs along the right side of the window to select the individual you want. However, after you have been researching for a while, you will discover that you have too many people in your files to do this effectively. In this chapter, you'll learn how to:

- Locate individuals using Quick Search
- Work with the Find feature
- Rearrange the index
- Search by name
- Search by other criteria
- Work in the FamilyFinder Center

Using Quick Search by Name

The Index of Individuals has a built-in quick search where you can easily type in the name of the individual for whom you are searching. This is the easiest way to locate an individual in your Family Tree file.

1. Click on **View**. The View menu will appear.

2. Click on **Index of Individuals**. The Index of Individuals dialog box will open.

TIP

There are two other ways to access the Index of Individuals dialog box. You can press the F2 key or click on the Index of Individuals button.

3. Click in the **Name field** and **type** the **surname** (last name) of the person you want to find. Family Tree Maker will move the highlight bar to different possible matches as you type.

NOTE

Notice that the highlight bar locates and moves to the first name that fits the letters you have entered. It is usually not necessary to type in the complete surname.

TIP

The Quick Search is not case sensitive. You can type the name in uppercase, lowercase, or mixed case.

Working with the Find Feature

There is a Find feature built into the Index of Individuals dialog box. This is an alternative for those times when the Quick Search is not available.

1. Press the **F2 key**. The Index of Individuals dialog box will open.

2. Click on the **Find button**. The Find Name dialog box will open.

3. In the Name field, **type** the **name** of the individual you want to find.

4. Click on **OK**. The Find Name dialog box will close and Family Tree Maker will highlight the first individual who fits your search.

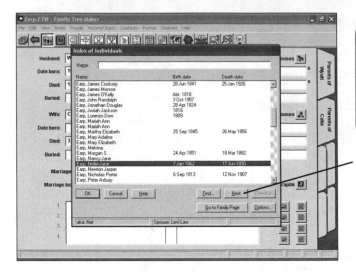

You do not need to type the entire name. You can type just the surname or the first name, and Family Tree Maker will go to the first individual with that name.

5. Click on **Next**. Family Tree Maker will highlight the next individual who fits your search.

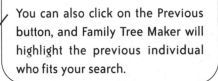

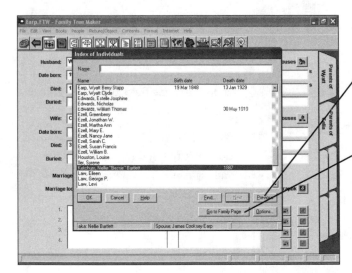

You can also click on the Previous button, and Family Tree Maker will highlight the previous individual who fits your search.

6. Click on the **Go to Family Page button**. The Index of Individuals dialog box will close and Family Tree Maker will display the Family Page for that individual.

If you are trying to return to a report or some other window, you will want to click on the OK button, which returns you to the window you were working in before you opened the Index of Individuals dialog box.

Rearranging the Index

The default arrangement of the Index of Individuals is alphabetical by last name in ascending order. However, you might want to view the list in a different format.

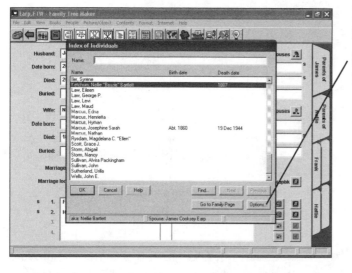

1. Press the **F2 key**. The Index of Individuals dialog box will open.

2. Click on **Options**. The Options dialog box will open.

3. Select a different **radio button** in the Sort individuals by list. This will change the order of the Index of Individuals.

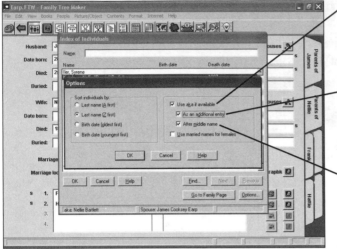

4. Click on the **Use aka if available check box** if you want the also known as name to display in the Index of Individuals.

5. Click on the **As an additional entry check box**. Family Tree Maker will create a new entry in the Index using the nickname.

6. Click on the **After middle name check box**. Family Tree Maker will add the nickname to the original Index entry, placing it after the individual's middle name.

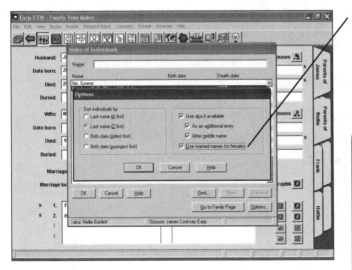

7. Click on the **Use married names for females check box**. Family Tree Maker will change the surname for each female in the index to display her married surname.

NOTE

Selecting the married names changes the surnames of all the females in the list so that they are listed by their married names instead of their maiden names, but it offers an easy way to list females for whom you don't have a maiden name.

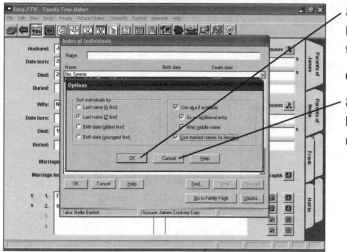

8a. Click on **OK**. The Options dialog box will close and your changes will take effect.

OR

8b. Click on **Cancel**. The Options dialog box will close, but the changes will not take effect.

NOTE

If you have changed the Sort individuals by option to something other than Last name (A first), the Quick Search Name field will be disabled.

Using the Find Individual Feature

While you will often search for an individual by name or by scrolling through the Index of Individuals, you might also need to look for individuals in a different manner. You can do this using the Find Individual feature.

1. Click on the **Family Page button**. The Family Page window will appear.

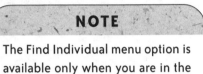

NOTE

The Find Individual menu option is available only when you are in the Family Page view.

2. Click on **Edit**. The Edit menu will appear.

3. Click on **Find Individual**. The Find Individual dialog box will open.

Searching by Name

You can use the Find Individual feature to search for individuals by name, perhaps looking for everyone who shares a similar given or middle name.

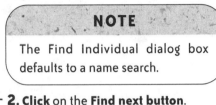

1. Type the **name** for which you want to search in the for field.

> **NOTE**
>
> The Find Individual dialog box defaults to a name search.

2. Click on the **Find next button**. Family Tree Maker will locate the first individual in the database with the name for which you are searching.

3. Click on the **Find next button** again. Family Tree Maker will display the next individual in the database with the name for which you are searching.

> **TIP**
>
> If you accidentally pass the individual you wanted, click on the **Find previous button** to go back in the search.

Searching by Date

At some point, you might want to determine who in your database was born or married prior to a specific date. The Find Individual feature has the ability to search by date.

1. Click on the **Search down arrow**. The Search drop-down menu will appear.

2. Click on the **Birth date option** and **press** the **Tab key**. The option will be selected and the cursor will move to the for field.

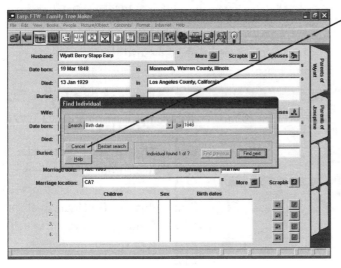

3. Type the **date** in the for field.

4. Click on the **Find next button**. Family Tree Maker will display the first Family Page window with a date that fits the search criteria.

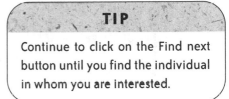

TIP

Continue to click on the Find next button until you find the individual in whom you are interested.

5. Click on **Cancel**. The Find Individual dialog box will close.

The following table shows you the many ways you can search for dates in your Family File.

If you type this	Family Tree Maker will find this
<10/2/1998, or BEFORE 10/2/1988, or BEF 10/2/1988	All dates before October 2, 1988, including dates entered as "Before October 2, 1988"
<=10/2/1988	The date October 2, 1988 and all dates before it, including dates entered as "Before October 2, 1988"
>10/2/1988, or AFTER 10/2/1988, or AFT 10/2/1988	All dates after October 2, 1988, including dates entered as "After October 2, 1988"
>=10/2/1988	The date October 2, 1988 and all dates after it, including dates entered as "After October 2, 1988"
ABOUT 10/2/1988, or CIRCA 10/2/1988, or EST 10/2/1988	All dates entered as "About October 2, 1988," "Circa October 2, 1988," or "Est October 2, 1988"
10/2/1988..10/2/1990, or >=10/2/1988..<=10/2/1990	All dates between October 2, 1988 and October 2, 1990, including those two days
>10/2/1988..<10/2/1990	All dates between October 2, 1988 and October 2, 1990, not including those two days
UNKNOWN or ?	All dates entered as "Unknown" or "?"

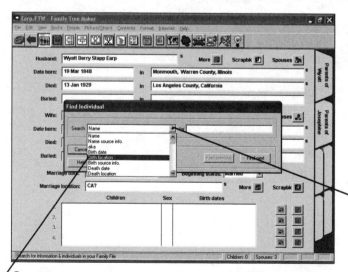

Searching by Location

After names and dates, the item in which researchers are most interested is location. The Find Individual feature allows you to search for a specific location.

1. Click on the **Search down arrow**. The Search drop-down menu will appear.

2. Click on the **Birth location option** and **press** the **Tab key**. The option will be selected and the cursor will move to the for field.

3. Type the **location** in the for field.

4. Click on the **Find next button**. Family Tree Maker will display the More About Facts screen for the first individual who fits the search criteria.

5. Continue to click on the **Find next button** until you find the individual in whom you are interested.

6. Click on **Cancel**. The Find Individual dialog box will close, and the More About Facts window for the last individual found will be displayed.

Searching by Source

You can also use the Find Individual feature to search for a specific source or to determine for which events and individuals you have cited a source.

1. Click on the **Search down arrow**. The Search drop-down menu will appear.

2. Click on the **Birth source info option** and **press** the **Tab key**. The option will be selected and the cursor will move to the for field.

TIP

Selecting Any and all text fields is a quick way to look through all text fields for a word.

3. Type the **word** for which you are looking in the for field.

4. Click on the **Find next button**. Family Tree Maker will display the first individual's record that contains the word for which you are searching.

NOTE

To see the text in question, you must open the More About window and look through the text fields.

Searching by Comment

You might be interested in discovering for which individuals you have entered medical information or other comments. You can do this using the Find Individual feature.

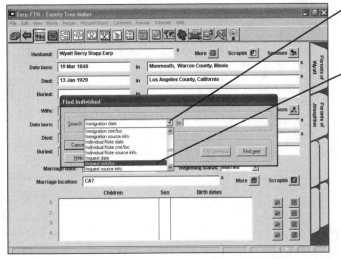

1. Click on the **Search down arrow**. The Search drop-down menu will appear.

2. Click on one of the **comment fields** in the menu and **press** the **Tab key**. The comment field you choose will appear in the Search field and the cursor will move to the for field.

3. Enter the **word** for which you want to search.

4. Click on the **Find next button**. Family Tree Maker will display the More About screen for the first person who fits the search criteria.

TIP

To find comments with any text, replace the word with !=, and Family Tree Maker will show you everyone who has any text in that comment field.

Working with the FamilyFinder Center

The FamilyFinder Center offers a number of different methods for searching and researching. At this point, we will concentrate on how to use the FamilyFinder Search and to view the generated report.

1. Click on the **FamilyFinder Center button**. The FamilyFinder Center will open.

2. Click on **Run a FamilyFinder Search**. A message box will appear, asking you whether you want to create a FamilyFinder Report.

3a. Click on **OK**. The message box will close and the Create New FamilyFinder Report dialog box will open.

OR

3b. Click on **Cancel**. A blank FamilyFinder Report will be displayed.

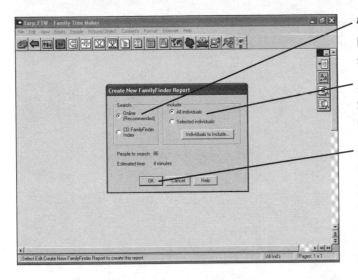

4. Select either **Online** or **CD FamilyFinder Index** in the Search section.

5. Select either **All individuals** or **Selected individuals** in the Include section.

6. Click on **OK**. If you are connected to the Internet, your browser will launch if you selected the Online option, which is the most thorough. When the search is complete, a message box will appear, telling you how many matches were found.

NOTE

If you click on the Individuals to Include button, the Individuals to Include dialog box will open. You might want to use this option when you have added some new individuals but you do not want the report to be rerun for everyone in the family file.

NOTE

See Chapter 14, "Working with Specialty Reports and the Research Journal," for more information on working with some of the other FamilyFinder Center options.

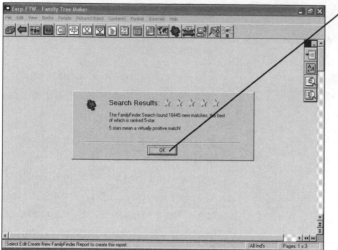

7. Click on **OK**. The FamilyFinder Report will be displayed.

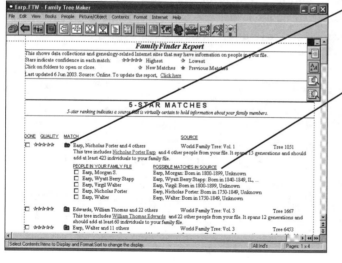

8. Click on the **file folder** for one of your matches. The FamilyFinder Report will give you more details about the match.

9. Click on the **possible match in source** and your browser will open and you will be taken to the appropriate online source.

NOTE

Some of the sources will require a subscription fee to access them.

10. Double-click on the **ancestor's name.** The Individual Facts Card for that individual will appear.

TIP

The more stars next to an entry, the higher the probability of the match being your ancestor.

NOTE

A star will appear on the Family Page next to anyone with a match in the FamilyFinder report.

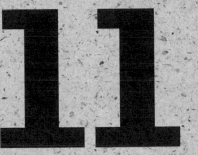

Correcting Information in Family Tree Maker

In a perfect world, every name and date you place in your Family Tree file would be accurate and you would never need to make any changes. However, since no one is infallible when entering data, Family Tree Maker offers ways to undo family relationships, check your spelling, and delete individuals. In this chapter, you'll learn how to:

- Use the spelling checker

- Undo a marriage

- Delete individuals from your Family Tree file

- Check for data entry errors

Working with the Family Tree Maker Spelling Checker

There are times when, in typing the details of a will or the place of birth based on a faded record, you might misspell words. However, you might not notice the error right away. Family Tree Maker includes a spelling checker to help remedy such problems.

Checking Spelling in the Entry Screens

You can ask Family Tree Maker to spell check all the notes and text items in a book from the entry screens and report windows.

1. Click on **Edit**. The Edit menu will appear.

2. Click on **Spell Check All**. The Spell Check dialog box will open and Family Tree Maker will move to the first Notes screen and highlight the first word not found in the dictionary.

CAUTION

It is important to understand that the spelling checker is going to go through all of your Notes screens when it is launched in this manner. If you have a significant number of notes this could take some time.

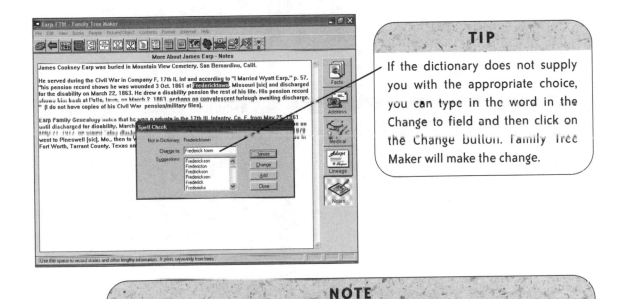

3a. Click on **Ignore** to ignore the word and move on in the spell check.

OR

3b. Click on **Change** to replace the highlighted word with the word listed in the Change to field.

OR

3c. Click on **Add** to place the highlighted word in the dictionary.

TIP

If the dictionary does not supply you with the appropriate choice, you can type in the word in the Change to field and then click on the Change button. Family Tree Maker will make the change.

NOTE

When the spelling checker highlights a word, it does not necessarily mean that the word is misspelled. It simply means that the word is not yet in the spelling checker's dictionary.

Checking Spelling in the Notes Windows

When you have finished entering the details in a More About Note or a More About Marriage Note, you might want to make a habit of running the spelling checker while you have the Notes window open.

1. In the Family Page window, **click** on the **More button**. The More About window will appear.

2. Click on the **Notes button**. The More About Notes window will appear.

TIP

Because the Menu Bar is disabled when you are working in the Individual Fact card, the only way to check the spelling in a Note is to use the More About sections available from the Family Page.

3. Click on **Edit**. The Edit menu will appear.

4. Click on **Spell Check Note**. The spelling checker will start.

Untying the Marriage Knot

As you continue with your research, you might discover that your information about a marriage is inaccurate. This is especially likely when you get into areas where you have multiple generations of the same name (for instance, John Smith, son of John Smith). Family Tree Maker includes options for undoing a marriage if you discover that the individuals you listed as married are not the correct two people.

1. Press the **F2 key**. The Index of Individuals dialog box will open.

2. Type the **name** of the individual for whom you need to untie a marriage.

3. Click on the correct **individual** in the list, if he or she is not already selected.

4. Click on **Go to Family Page**. The Family Page window for the selected individual will appear.

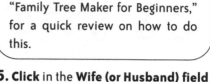

5. **Click** in the **Wife (or Husband) field** for the spouse you want to detach.

6. **Click** on **People**. The People menu will appear.

7. **Move** the **mouse pointer** to Fix Relationship Mistakes. The Fix Relationship Mistakes menu will appear.

8. **Click** on **Detach Spouse**. Family Tree Maker will open a message box, verifying that you want to detach the spouse.

9. **Click** on **OK** to confirm the change.

Removing People from Your Family File

Detaching a spouse removes the individual from the marriage, but it does not remove the individual from your Family Tree file. However, you might discover that you do have an Individual or group that needs to be deleted completely from the database.

Deleting a Single Person

When you discover a single individual who should be removed from the database, you can delete that person in the Family Page window.

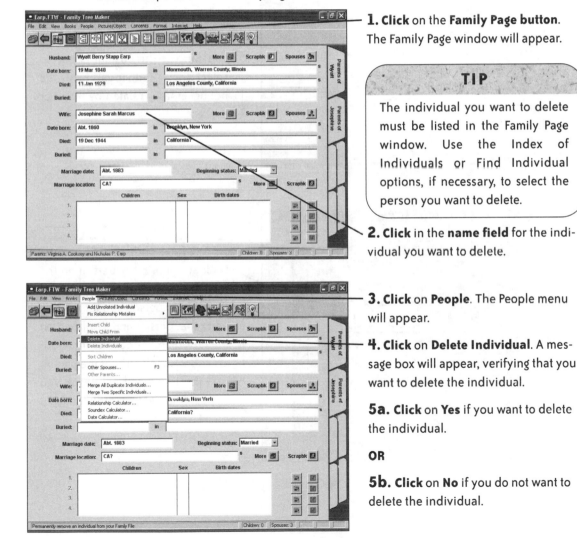

1. Click on the **Family Page button**. The Family Page window will appear.

> **TIP**
>
> The individual you want to delete must be listed in the Family Page window. Use the Index of Individuals or Find Individual options, if necessary, to select the person you want to delete.

2. Click in the **name field** for the individual you want to delete.

3. Click on **People**. The People menu will appear.

4. Click on **Delete Individual**. A message box will appear, verifying that you want to delete the individual.

5a. Click on **Yes** if you want to delete the individual.

OR

5b. Click on **No** if you do not want to delete the individual.

Deleting a Group of People

If you want to delete a group of individuals, you can select them via the Tree views and the Custom Report. The group of individuals to be deleted must be visible on the report in order for you to delete them as a group.

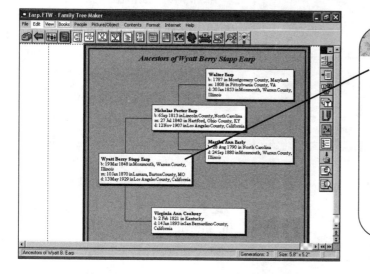

1. Click on a **Tree button**. The selected Tree menu will appear.

2. Click on a **Tree style**. The appropriate Tree window will appear.

> ### NOTE
>
> You can use the Custom Report to select those individuals who are not necessarily related by blood or descent.

> ### NOTE
>
> Look at the primary person on the report. It is important to verify that the primary person and those related to that person and displayed on the report are indeed the individuals you wish to delete. If the person isn't the individual you want, you can use the Index of Individuals to select a new person.

3. Click on the **Index of Individuals button**. The Index of Individuals dialog box will open.

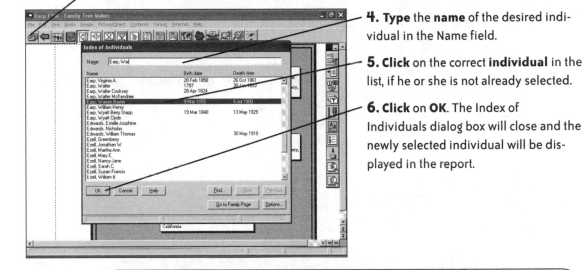

4. Type the **name** of the desired individual in the Name field.

5. Click on the correct **individual** in the list, if he or she is not already selected.

6. Click on **OK**. The Index of Individuals dialog box will close and the newly selected individual will be displayed in the report.

TIP

Some of the reports allow you to include siblings. You will learn more about this in Chapter 13 "Looking at the Tree Reports in Family Tree Maker."

---

7. Click on **People**. The People menu will appear.

8. Click on **Delete Individuals in Ancestor Tree**. A message box will appear, verifying that you do indeed want to delete the individuals from your Family File. The actual wording of this menu item will differ, depending on the type of report or tree you selected.

NOTE

Remember that **everyone** who shows up on the report or tree displayed will be deleted. This is not how you delete a single person. See the previous section of this chapter to see how to delete one individual.

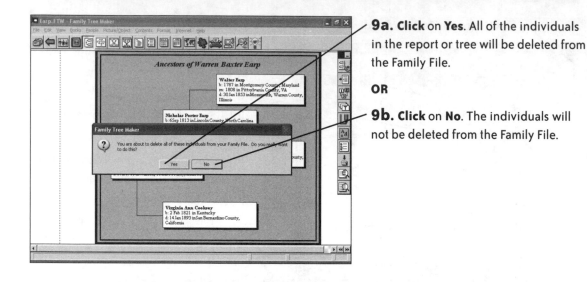

9a. **Click** on **Yes**. All of the individuals in the report or tree will be deleted from the Family File.

OR

9b. **Click** on **No**. The individuals will not be deleted from the Family File.

CAUTION

Deleting individuals from the Family File becomes permanent as soon as you move on to something else in the program. You have one chance directly after removing the individuals to bring them back using the Undo feature found under the Edit menu. If you are not familiar with this feature, you should create a backup of your family file before deleting anyone. You can learn more about backup files in Chapter 21 "Working with GEDCOM Files and Other Family Files."

Checking the Family File for Errors

Family Tree Maker offers you three different ways to scan your Family File for errors. One is automatic, another runs a scan when you request it, and the third is a report of the errors that Family Tree Maker has found.

Data Entry Checking

Family Tree Maker offers a feature that works automatically after it is turned on. This data entry checking feature will let you know when you have entered what Family Tree Maker thinks is a questionable date or name error.

1. Click on **File**. The File menu will appear.

2. Click on **Preferences**. The Preferences dialog box will open.

3. Click on the **Name errors check box**. Family Tree Maker will check for name errors.

4. Click on the **Unlikely birth, death, and marriage dates check box**. Family Tree Maker will check for date errors.

5. Click on **OK**. The Error Checking dialog box will close.

NOTE

When you type in a date that doesn't coincide with the other dates for an individual or family, Family Tree Maker will open a Data Entry Error message box to point out the problem.

Using the Find Error Command

The Find Error command is like a spelling checker for the dates that have been entered. It identifies the errors and then allows you to fix or skip each error. Be sure you are in the Family Page, as this is the only screen in the program where the Find Error command is available.

1. Click on **Edit**. The Edit menu will appear.

2. Click on **Find Error**. The Find Error dialog box will open.

3. Select the **errors** for which you want to search. You can search for name errors and/or unlikely birth, death, and marriage dates by selecting the appropriate check box.

4. Click on **OK**. Family Tree Maker will search your Family File for errors. When an error is found, you will have several options.

NOTE

The Reset all ignored errors button allows you to overwrite the Ignore Error check box you will be introduced to in the next set of steps.

5a. Click on the **Find next button**. Family Tree Maker will bypass the error and find the next one.

OR

5b. Click on the **AutoFix button**. Family Tree Maker will change the error based on where it thinks the information should be placed.

OR

5c. Click on the **Ignore error check box**. Family Tree Maker will ignore the error now (and in the future, if you want it to).

NOTE

If you turn on the Ignore error check box, Family Tree Maker will ignore the error each time you run Find Error until you click on the Reset all ignored errors button at the start of the Find Error search. The Ignore error check box can be used to have Family Tree Maker bypass those idiosyncrasies unique to the names or dates you are entering.

TIP

If you selected AutoFix in error, or if the change made by Family Tree Maker is not correct, click on Undo. If you use the Undo feature, you will not move to the next error until you click on the Find next button.

Working with the Data Errors Report

From time to time it is a good idea to run the Data Errors Report. This lists all the potential errors that Family Tree Maker identifies in your Family File. After printing this report, you can take time to read through it and determine what in your Family File you might need to change.

1. Click on **View**. The View menu will appear.

2. Move the **mouse pointer** to Reports. The Reports submenu will appear.

3. Click on **Data Errors**. The Data Errors Report window will appear.

4. Click on an **individual** to highlight that person in the list. Notice the potential error.

5. Double-click on the **individual** to edit his or her information. The Individual Facts Card for that individual will appear.

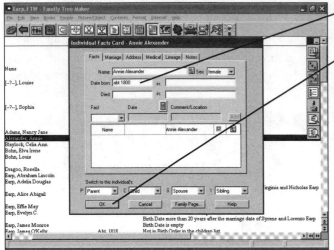

6. Correct the **error** in the Individual Facts Card.

7. Click on **OK** to return to the Data Errors Report to work on the next error. The Data Errors Report will reappear.

12

Fixing Relationships & Duplicates

Sometimes, after you have imported a cousin's GEDCOM or data from World Family Tree, you will discover that you have duplicate entries for individuals. At other times, you might find that you need to adjust the relationship between a child and the parents. In this chapter, you'll learn how to:

- Link children to their parents
- Detach a child from the wrong parents
- Link individuals by marriage
- Merge duplicates
- Search and replace

Fixing Relationships

There will be times when it is necessary to change relationships between individuals in your Family File. Family Tree Maker recognizes that, as your research progresses, you will discover an error in how you have connected individuals in a family structure.

Linking Children to Their Parents

You might discover that you already have a child and his or her parents entered in your Family File, but you did not realize they were related when you originally entered them. It's easy to link children to parents in Family Tree Maker.

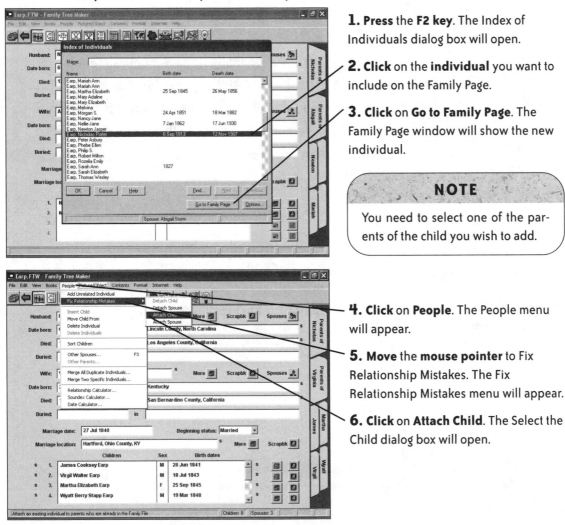

1. Press the **F2 key**. The Index of Individuals dialog box will open.

2. Click on the **individual** you want to include on the Family Page.

3. Click on **Go to Family Page**. The Family Page window will show the new individual.

NOTE

You need to select one of the parents of the child you wish to add.

---

4. Click on **People**. The People menu will appear.

5. Move the **mouse pointer** to Fix Relationship Mistakes. The Fix Relationship Mistakes menu will appear.

6. Click on **Attach Child**. The Select the Child dialog box will open.

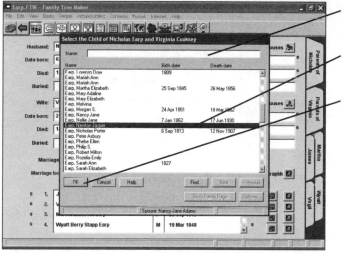

7. Type the **name** of the individual you want to add as a child.

8. Click on the **name** of the individual in the list.

9. Click on **OK**. A message box will appear, verifying that you want to attach the individual as a child on the Family Page.

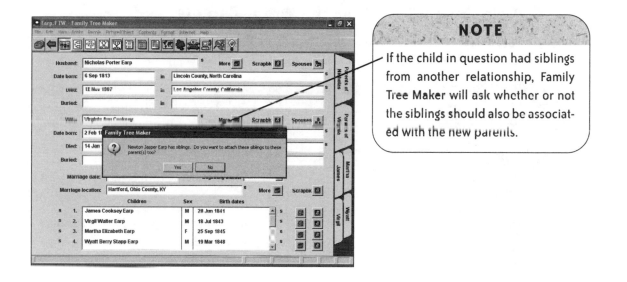

NOTE

If the child in question had siblings from another relationship, Family Tree Maker will ask whether or not the siblings should also be associated with the new parents.

10a. Click on **Yes**. The child will be added to the Family Page.

OR

10b. Click on **No**. The child will not be added to the Family Page.

Detaching a Child from the Wrong Parents

If you discover that a child has been linked to the wrong parents, you can easily detach the child from that family. This will not delete the child from the Family File.

1. Press F2. The Index of Individuals dialog box will open.

2. Type the **name** of one of the parents in the Name field.

3. Click on the correct **name** in the list.

4. Click on **Go to Family Page**. The family will be displayed in the Family Page window.

5. Click on the **child** you want to detach in the Children list.

6. Click on **People**. The People menu will appear.

7. Move the **mouse pointer** to Fix Relationship Mistakes. The Fix Relationship Mistakes menu will appear.

8. Click on **Detach Child**. A message box will appear, asking if you want to detach the siblings of the selected individual as well.

9a. Click on **Yes**. The siblings of the child will also be detached.

OR

9b. Click on **No**. The siblings of the child will not be detached.

> **NOTE**
>
> The final message box will verify that you do indeed wish to detach the child from the family. Answering yes will detach the child. Answering no will leave the child where he or she is in the family.

Linking Individuals by Marriage

Unlike typing in the names of two spouses in the Family Page view, the steps for linking two previously entered individuals require picking one of the individuals out of a list.

1. Click on **View**. The View menu will appear.

2. Click on **Index of Individuals**. The Index of Individuals dialog box will open.

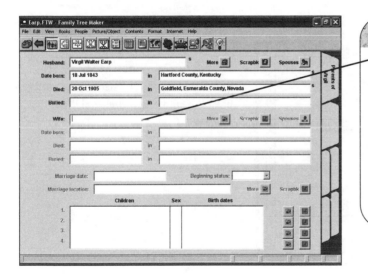

3. Click on the **individual** you want as one of the spouses.

4. Click on **Go to Family Page**. The Family Page window will appear.

NOTE

There must be a place for the new spouse to go. That means that in the Family Page, the spouse field must be empty. If the individual in question already has a spouse, you need to use the Spouses button to add the spouse. See Chapter 3, "Family Tree Maker for Beginners," for a quick review of how to do that.

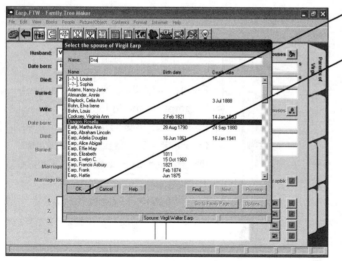

5. Click on **People**. The People menu will appear.

6. Move the **mouse pointer** to Fix Relationship Mistakes. The Fix Relationship Mistakes menu will appear.

7. Click on **Attach Spouse**. The Select the spouse dialog box will open.

8. Click on the **name** of the individual you want to select as the spouse.

9. Click on **OK**. A message box will appear, asking if you're sure you want to make the selected individual the spouse.

10a. Click on **Yes**. The spouse will be attached.

OR

10b. Click on **No**. The spouse will not be attached.

Fixing Duplicates

Often, when you are adding information from a fellow researcher, you will end up with duplicate individuals in your Family File. Sometimes the duplication is the result of entering an individual twice.

Using the Merge Duplicate Individuals Function

Family Tree Maker offers a method to merge individuals that looks not only at the name of the individuals, but also at additional information, such as family relationships and dates of events. You must be in the Family Page for the Merge Duplicates options to be enabled on the People menu.

1. Click on **People**. The People menu will appear.

2. Click on **Merge All Duplicate Individuals**. A message box will appear, reminding you to back up your file before you merge duplicate individuals.

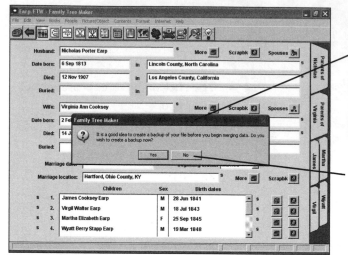

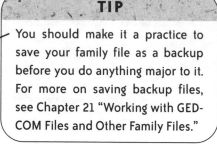

TIP

You should make it a practice to save your family file as a backup before you do anything major to it. For more on saving backup files, see Chapter 21 "Working with GED-COM Files and Other Family Files."

3. Click on **No**. The Merge All Duplicate Individuals dialog box will open.

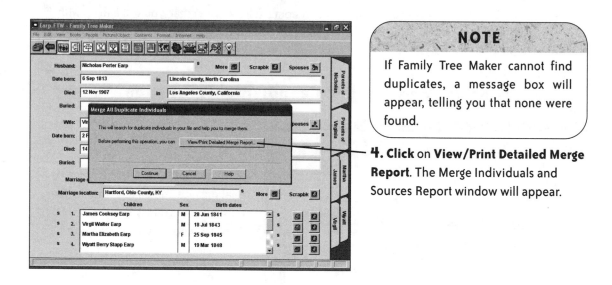

NOTE

If Family Tree Maker cannot find duplicates, a message box will appear, telling you that none were found.

4. Click on **View/Print Detailed Merge Report**. The Merge Individuals and Sources Report window will appear.

Merge Individuals and Sources Report

This is a complete description of the merge operation.

Individual 1	Individual 2	Comments/Differences
Likely Matches	Will Check before Merging with...	
Hattie Earp, b. Jun 1873	Hattie Earp, b. Jun 1873	Street 1
		City
		State or province
		Zip or postal code
		Country
		Phone
		Additional relationship: p
Mariah Ann Earp	Mariah Ann Earp	Parent has different or no

Individual #1: Street 602 7th Street
Individual #2: Street

TIP

You can click on a line in the list to get some additional information about the differences between the two possible duplicates.

5. Click on **Close**. The Merge All Duplicate Individuals dialog box will reappear.

NOTE

If you have a particularly lengthy list of potential duplicates, it is a good idea to print out this report before going ahead with the additional steps. This way you have a printed record of the duplicates Family Tree Maker merged.

6. Click on **Continue**. The Likely Matches dialog box will open with all matches selected for merging.

Husband: Nicholas Porter Earp
Date born: 6 Sep 1813 in Lincoln County, North Carolina
Died: 12 Nov 1907 in Los Angeles County, California
Buried:

Merge All Duplicate Individuals

This will search for duplicate individuals in your file and help you to merge them.

Before performing this operation, you can [View/Print Detailed Merge Report...]

[Continue] [Cancel] [Help]

Marriage location: Hartford, Ohio County, KY

	Children	Sex	Birth dates
s	1. James Cooksey Earp	M	28 Jun 1841
s	2. Virgil Walter Earp	M	18 Jul 1843
s	3. Martha Elizabeth Earp	F	25 Sep 1845
s	4. Wyatt Berry Stapp Earp	M	19 Mar 1848

> **NOTE**
>
> Family Tree Maker uses the check boxes next to the potential duplicates to select them for action.

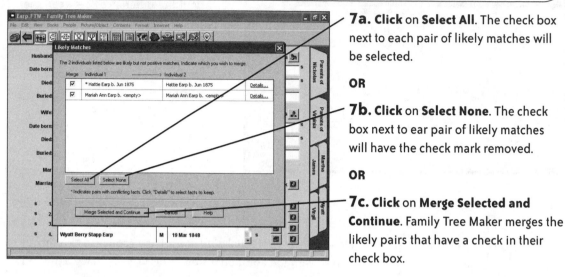

7a. Click on **Select All**. The check box next to each pair of likely matches will be selected.

OR

7b. Click on **Select None**. The check box next to ear pair of likely matches will have the check mark removed.

OR

7c. Click on **Merge Selected and Continue**. Family Tree Maker merges the likely pairs that have a check in their check box.

OR

7d. Click on **Cancel**. The Likely Matches dialog box will close and the merge will be cancelled.

8. Click on **Details**. The Merge Individuals dialog box will open.

> **NOTE**
>
> The Merge Individuals details dialog box is a great way to compare information between the two before telling Family Tree Maker to merge everything.

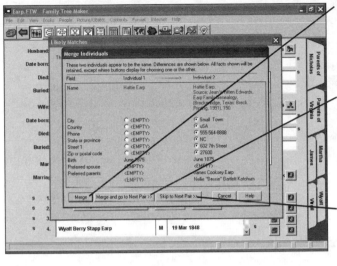

9a. Click on **Merge**. The individuals will be merged and the Merge Individuals dialog box will close.

OR

9b. Click on **Merge and go to Next Pair**. The individuals will be merged and the details for the next pair of individuals in the Likely Matches dialog box will be shown.

OR

9c. Click on **Skip to Next Pair**. The individuals will not be merged and the details for the next pair of individuals in the Likely Matches dialog box will be shown.

OR

9d. Click on **Cancel**. The individuals will not be merged and the Merge Individuals dialog box will close.

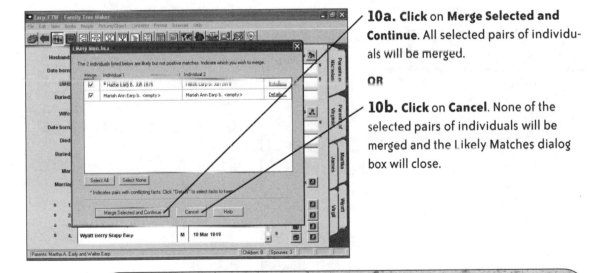

10a. Click on **Merge Selected and Continue**. All selected pairs of individuals will be merged.

OR

10b. Click on **Cancel**. None of the selected pairs of individuals will be merged and the Likely Matches dialog box will close.

NOTE

Family Tree Maker will remind you that by canceling the merge, your file will be restored to the way it was before you began to merge anyone. Click on OK to close this message box.

Merging Specific Individuals

There are times when you will want total control over the individuals you wish to select for merging. You gain this control using the Merge Specific Individuals menu option.

1. Press F2. The Index of Individuals dialog box will open.

2. Select one **individual** you wish to merge.

3. Click on **OK**. The Family Page view will open.

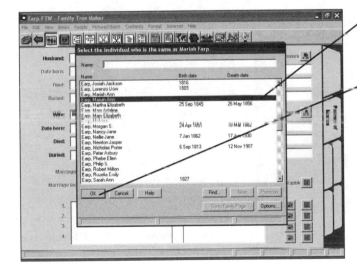

4. Click on **People**. The People menu will appear.

5. Click on **Merge Two Specific Individuals**. The Select the individual who is the same as dialog box will open.

6. Click on the **name** of the person with whom you wish to merge the first individual.

7. Click on **OK**. A message box will appear, verifying that the individuals should be merged.

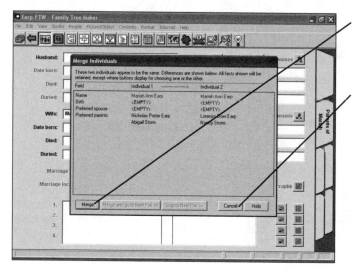

8a. Click on **Yes**. The Merge Individuals dialog box will open.

OR

8b. Click on **No**. The merge function will be canceled.

9a. Click on **Merge**. The two individuals will be merged.

OR

9b. Click on **Cancel**. The two individuals will not be merged.

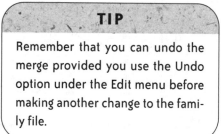

TIP

Remember that you can undo the merge provided you use the Undo option under the Edit menu before making another change to the family file.

Using Global Find and Replace

You may discover that you have consistently misspelled a word or phrase. The Find and Replace feature allows you to have Family Tree Maker search for the wrong word or phrase and replace it with the correct word or phrase. Like many of the other features we have looked at in this chapter, you must start out in the Family Page.

2. Click on **Edit**. The Edit menu will appear.

3. Click on **Find and Replace**. The Find and Replace dialog box will open.

4. In the Find field, **enter** the **word or phrase** you want to find.

5. In the Replace with field, **type** the **word or phrase** with which you want to replace it.

6. Click on **Find**. The Find and Replace dialog box will show the first match.

7a. Click on **Replace All**. Family Tree Maker will replace all occurrences of the Find word with the Replace with word.

OR

7b. Click on **Replace**. Family Tree Maker will replace just that particular occurrence of the Find word with the Replace with word.

OR

7c. Click on **Find Next**. Family Tree Maker will ignore the current occurrence and look for the next match.

8. Click on **Close**. Family Tree Maker will close the Find and Replace dialog box.

PART

IV

Getting to Know Family Tree Maker Trees and Reports

Chapter 13
   Looking at Tree Reports . .193

Chapter 14
   Specialty Reports and the
   Research Journal 217

Chapter 15
   Viewing and Printing Reports
   and Trees 237

Chapter 16
   Creating Genealogy Style
   and Genealogical Source
   Reports 245

Looking at the Tree Reports in Family Tree Maker

After you have entered information about your family into Family Tree Maker, it is natural for you to want to display that information in different formats. Family Tree Maker offers a number of different trees that will show your ancestors, descendants, or both for a selected individual. In this chapter, you'll learn how to:

- Display Ancestor Trees
- Display Hourglass Trees
- Display Descendant Trees
- Display All-in-One Trees
- Enhance the Tree views

Displaying Ancestor Trees

The Ancestor Trees allow you to see how many direct line generations you have been able to carry your research back from a selected individual. Family Tree Maker offers three different versions of the Ancestor Tree.

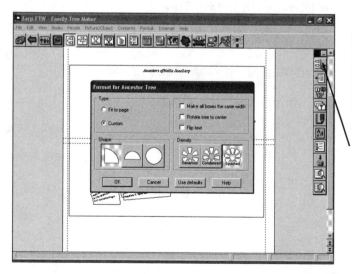

Creating Fan Charts

The Fan Chart of an Ancestor Tree begins with the selected individual. It then displays all the ancestors: parents, grandparents, great-grandparents, and so on. You can control how the chart looks and how many generations to include.

1. Click on the **Ancestor Tree button**. The Ancestor Tree menu will appear.

2. Click on **Fan**. The Fan Chart will appear.

> **TIP**
>
> Family Tree Maker allows you to change the format of the chart using the toolbar along the right side of the tree.

3. Click on the **Format button**. The Format for Ancestor Tree dialog box will open.

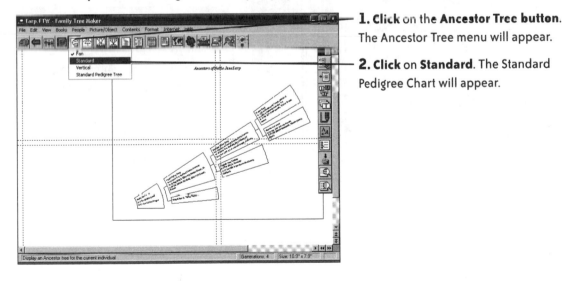

4. Select the **Custom radio button**. All the options will be enabled.

5. Select the **shape** of the Fan Chart.

6. Select the **density** of the Fan Chart.

7. Click on **OK**. The Format for Ancestor Tree dialog box will close and your changes will be displayed.

NOTE

Throughout this chapter, you will examine all the different toolbar buttons as you learn about each tree.

Creating a Pedigree Chart

The pedigree chart is the standard chart used by genealogists. This chart is a road map of your direct lineage and usually displays from four to six generations per page.

1. Click on the **Ancestor Tree button**. The Ancestor Tree menu will appear.

2. Click on **Standard**. The Standard Pedigree Chart will appear.

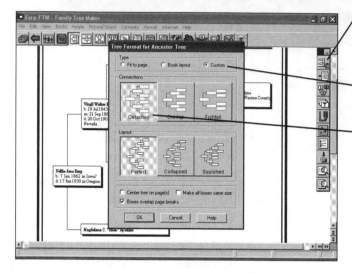

3. Click on the **Format button**. The Tree Format for Ancestor Tree dialog box will open.

4. Select the **type of Ancestor Tree** you want to display.

5. Select the **type of connections** you want to use in the chart. The chart's boxes will be moved closer together or farther apart, depending on the type of connections you select.

NOTE

The Layout options are only active when you select the Custom type.

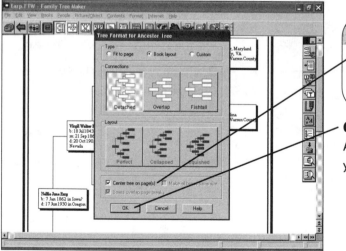

TIP

When you select the Book layout or custom type, you can elect to have each tree centered on the page.

6. Click on **OK**. The Tree Format for Ancestor Tree dialog box will close and your changes will be displayed.

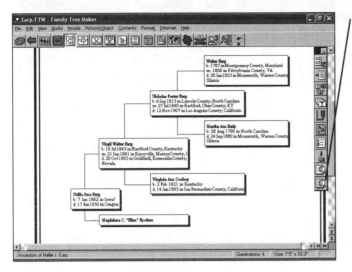

7. Click on the **Zoom Out button**. You will see more of the tree.

Rearranging the Standard Ancestor Chart

While the Ancestor Tree is a standard form, better known as a pedigree chart, many researchers are finding they like to customize the chart. In addition to the methods mentioned above, you can also move individual boxes or a complete lineage using your mouse and the keyboard.

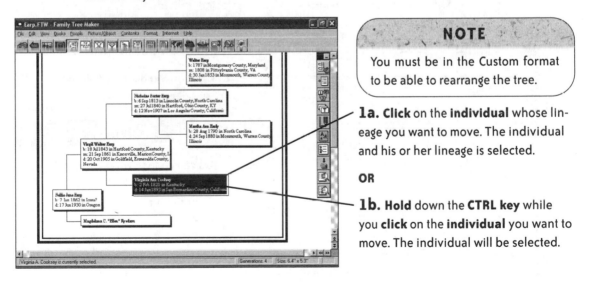

NOTE

You must be in the Custom format to be able to rearrange the tree.

1a. Click on the **individual** whose lineage you want to move. The individual and his or her lineage is selected.

OR

1b. Hold down the **CTRL key** while you **click** on the **individual** you want to move. The individual will be selected.

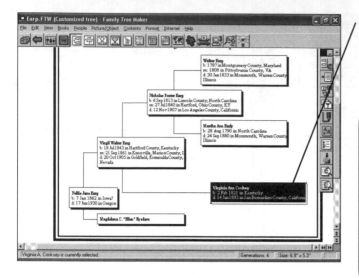

2. Drag the **mouse** to the new location. The individual or the selected lineage will be moved elsewhere on the chart that you have selected.

NOTE

Remember that when you are dragging the mouse, it is necessary to hold down the left mouse button or the left mouse button and the CTRL key to achieve the desired effect of either moving the lineage of an individual or just moving the individual selected.

Creating a Vertical Ancestor Tree

The Vertical Ancestor Tree is a box-style chart. It starts at the bottom of a page or set of pages and goes up, showing the ancestors of the selected individual.

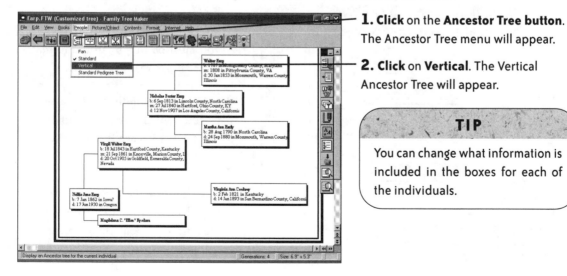

1. Click on the **Ancestor Tree button**. The Ancestor Tree menu will appear.

2. Click on **Vertical**. The Vertical Ancestor Tree will appear.

TIP

You can change what information is included in the boxes for each of the individuals.

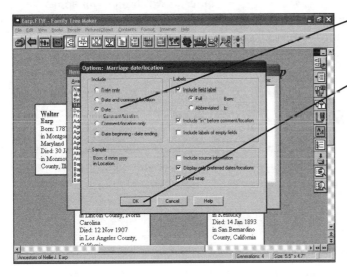

3. Click on the **Items to Include button**. The Items to Include in Ancestor Tree dialog box will open.

4. Click on an **item** in the Available items list.

5. Click on the **Inclusion button**. The Options dialog box will open.

6. Click on the **options** for the selected item. A check mark will appear next to the options selected.

7. Click on **OK**. The Options dialog box will close and the item will appear in the The boxes in your tree contain these items list.

NOTE

The choices in the Options dialog box will vary depending on the item you selected from the Available items list.

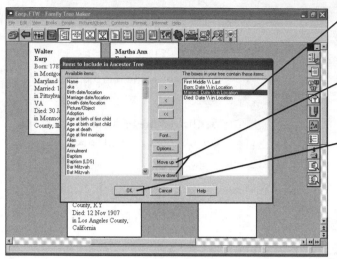

8. Click on an **item** in the The boxes in your tree contain these items list. The item will be selected.

9. Click on the **Move up or Move down button**. The item will be moved to a new position.

10. Click on **OK**. The changes will be applied to the Vertical Ancestor Tree.

> **NOTE**
>
> The order in which the items appear in the The boxes in your tree contain these items list is the order in which they will appear in the boxes of the tree.

Including Siblings on Trees

Once in a while you might want to get a good overall view of your data with more than just the direct ancestral lineage. Taking advantage of the option to include siblings is one way to do that. Before beginning these steps, make sure you have the Vertical Ancestor Tree open.

> **NOTE**
>
> While this example concentrates on the Vertical Ancestor Tree, this option is available for all of the Ancestor Tree formats, as well as for the Standard Hourglass Tree.

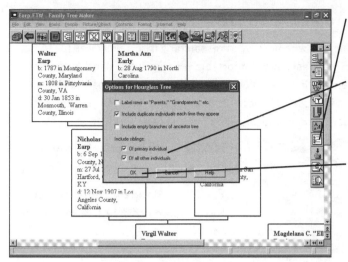

1. Click on the **Options button**. The Options for Ancestor Tree dialog box will open.

2. Click on the **Include siblings check box** for the siblings you wish to add to the Vertical Ancestor Tree. A check mark will appear in the selected box.

3. Click on **OK**. The Options for Ancestor Tree dialog box will close.

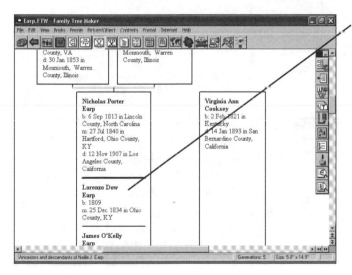

Notice how the changes affect the overall look of the Vertical Ancestor Tree, especially if you have elected to include the siblings for everyone on the tree.

Sharing the Standard Pedigree Tree

If you are sharing with genealogists who have been researching their family tree for some time, it is possible that they would feel more comfortable with a printed standard pedigree tree. This tree resembles the forms that genealogists have been using for many years, including having blank spaces for cousins to add information and return to you. You can even number it using a standard format recognized by other researchers.

1. Click on the **Ancestor Tree button**. The Ancestor Tree menu will appear.

2. Click on **Standard Pedigree Tree**. The Standard Pedigree Tree report will appear.

TIP

The Standard Pedigree Tree report allows you to send a report when communicating with a fellow researcher so that they can supply you with information you may not have known.

NOTE

When you are in the Standard Pedigree Tree, the Family Tree Templates is disabled. You will learn more about this feature of the tree reports in "Enhancing Your Tree with Templates" in Chapter 15.

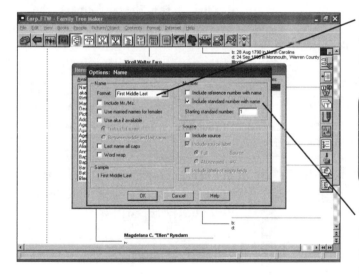

3. Click on the **Items to Include button**. The Items to Include dialog box will open.

4. Click on the **Name** in the The boxes in your tree contain column. The Name item will be highlighted.

5. Click on **Options**. The Options: Name dialog box will open.

6. Select a **name format** from the pull down list. The name format will be selected.

> ### NOTE
>
> When sharing with other researchers, it is a good idea to adhere to the standards, including capitalizing the surname.

7. Click on the **Include standard number with name** check box. The option will be selected and then be sure that the starting number is a 1.

> ### NOTE
>
> A standard pedigree tree identifies the individuals in the tree with numbers. The first person on each chart is a number 1, with reference back to that person on a previous chart.

Displaying Hourglass Trees

The Hourglass Tree allows you to view not only the ancestors but also the descendants of the selected individual. The individual is in the center with the ancestors opening above and the descendants opening below, in a pattern that resembles an hourglass.

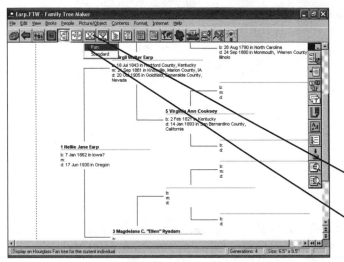

Working with Fan Format

Like other fan-styled trees, the Hourglass Tree in fan format takes advantage of the fan shape. Keep in mind that with a large lineage, the fan style will use up a lot of paper when you print it.

1. Click on the **Hourglass Tree button**. The Hourglass Tree menu will appear.

2. Click on **Fan**. The fan format of the Hourglass Tree will appear.

TIP

If the primary individual isn't the one that you want, you can use the Index of Individuals dialog box, available in the View menu or by pressing F2, to select a different individual. See Chapter 10, "Searching Your Family Tree File," to review how to do this.

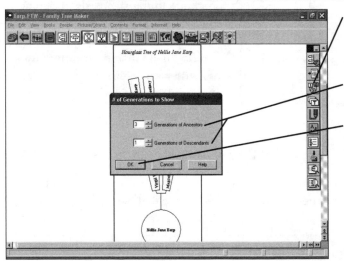

3. Click on the **Number of Generations button**. The # of Generations to Show dialog box will open.

4. Use the **arrows** to select the number of ancestors and descendants desired.

5. Click on **OK**. The # of Generations to Show dialog box will close.

Working with Standard Format

The standard format of the Hourglass Tree uses a box chart. The boxes can be as large or as small as you want, depending on the information you include. Remember that the more information you elect to include the fewer individuals will fit on a given page.

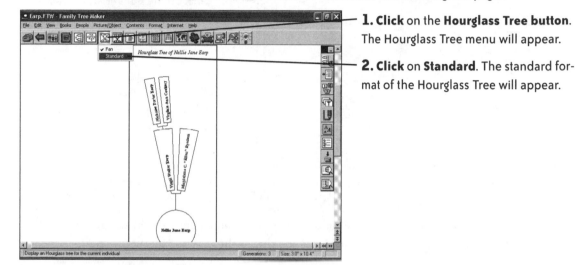

1. Click on the **Hourglass Tree button**. The Hourglass Tree menu will appear.

2. Click on **Standard**. The standard format of the Hourglass Tree will appear.

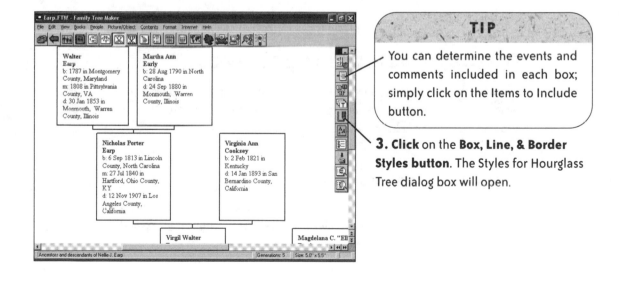

TIP

You can determine the events and comments included in each box; simply click on the Items to Include button.

3. Click on the **Box, Line, & Border Styles button**. The Styles for Hourglass Tree dialog box will open.

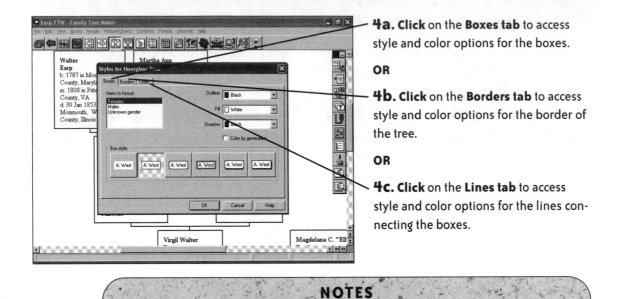

4a. Click on the **Boxes tab** to access style and color options for the boxes.

OR

4b. Click on the **Borders tab** to access style and color options for the border of the tree.

OR

4c. Click on the **Lines tab** to access style and color options for the lines connecting the boxes.

NOTES

Each of these sections uses buttons and drop-down menus to make the options available. It is through these options that you change the look and feel of the chart.

Displaying Descendant Trees

There will be times when you want to view the descendants of a given ancestor. Some research projects will require tracing the children and grandchildren. Descendant Trees allow you to see these in an easy-to-read format.

Creating a Standard Tree

As with the other trees you have looked at, there is a standard format of the Descendant Tree. This standard tree is often known as a box chart. It details the descendants of a selected individual.

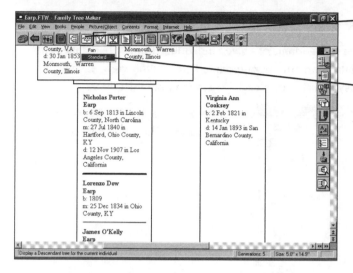

1. Click on the **Descendant Tree button**. The Descendant Tree menu will appear.

2. Click on **Standard**. The standard format of the Descendant Tree will appear.

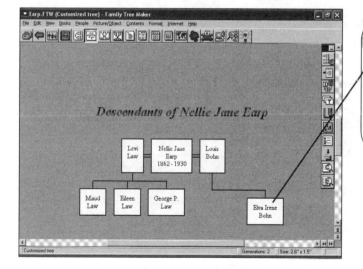

TIP

You can rearrange the shape of the Standard Descendant Tree by clicking and dragging, as you did with the Standard Ancestor Tree earlier in this chapter.

Creating an Outline Tree

When you're working with the descendants of a given individual, Family Tree Maker offers the capability to view your data as an outline, or indented, tree. In this view, each generation is indented, making it easy to distinguish each generation from the others.

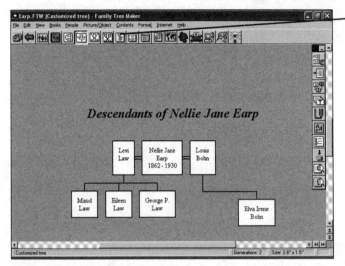

1. Click on the **Outline Descendant Tree button**. The Outline Report will appear.

2. Click on the **Format button**. The Tree Format for Outline Descendant Tree dialog box will open.

NOTE

This dialog box allows you to change the indent character as well as its size and spacing.

3. Click on **OK**. The Tree Format for Outline Descendant Tree dialog box will close.

Displaying All-in-One Trees

There will be times when you will want to view all the individuals in your database. Family Tree Maker makes this possible with the All-in-One Tree.

Creating an All-in-One Tree

An All-in-One Tree is easily created because Family Tree Maker does all the hard work.

1. Click on the **All-in-One Tree button**. The All-in-One Tree will appear.

2. Click on the **Options button**. The Options for All-in-One Tree dialog box will open.

NOTE

The dotted lines you see on the All-in-One Tree display the page margins. The All-in-One Tree will require multiple pages when printed, and those pages will then need to be taped together.

TIP

The Unconnected Branches check boxes allow you to include or exclude unconnected lines that have been entered in your database.

3. **Choose** your desired **settings** and **click** on **OK**. The Options for All-in-One Tree dialog box will close.

Setting Display Size

Because the All-in-One Tree displays all the individuals in your database, its size can be cumbersome. Customizing the display size can make it easier to understand the true scope of this view.

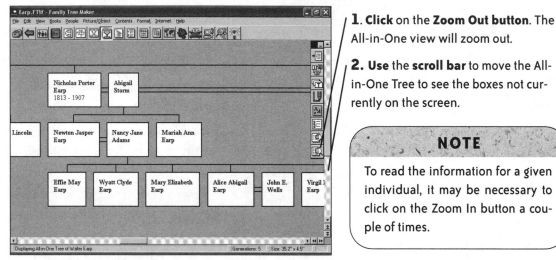

1. **Click** on the **Zoom Out button**. The All-in-One view will zoom out.

2. **Use** the **scroll bar** to move the All-in-One Tree to see the boxes not currently on the screen.

NOTE

To read the information for a given individual, it may be necessary to click on the Zoom In button a couple of times.

TIP

You can also select the Zoom option from the View menu. To see the entire All-in-One Tree, choose Size to Window.

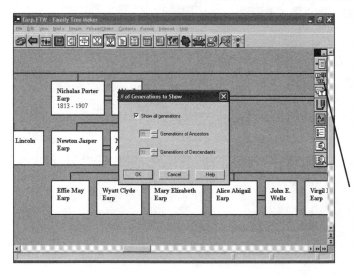

Pruning the Display

In addition to excluding the unrelated trees, you can control the number of generations included in your tree, by selecting the number of generations you want displayed of the ancestors and descendants of the primary person.

1. **Click** on the **Number of Generations button**. The # of Generations to Show dialog box will open.

2. Click on the **Show all generations check box** to clear it.

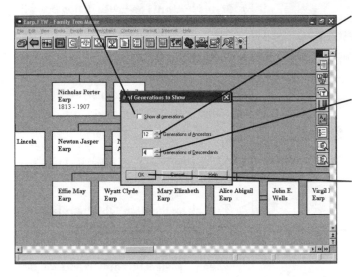

3. Use the **arrows** in the Generations of Ancestors field to select the number of generations of ancestors you want to show.

4. Use the **arrows** in the Generations of Descendants field to select the number of generations of descendants you want to show.

5. Click on **OK**. The # of Generations to Show dialog box will close and the changes will appear on the tree.

TIP

A quick way to change the number of generations of ancestors or descendants is to double click on the number of generations to highlight it and then type in the new number.

Enhancing Tree Views

There are different ways to enhance the appearance of the different trees. With colors and different box styles, you can make different lineages or genders stand out. The Descendant Tree report is one that benefits from these types of enhancements.

Emphasizing Relationships

With line styles and colors, you can make a particular relationship clearer on your tree.

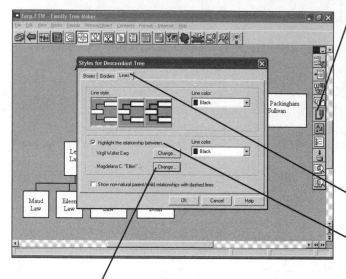

1. Click on the **Box, Line, & Border Styles button**. The Styles dialog box will open.

NOTE

The exact name of the Styles dialog box will vary, depending on what type of tree you are enhancing.

---

2. Click on the **Lines tab**. The Lines tab will move to the front.

3. Click on the **Highlight the relationship between check box** to select or deselect it. A check mark will appear when you select this option and will disappear when you deselect it.

4. Click on the **Change button** to change one of the individuals currently selected. The Index of Individuals dialog box will open and will include a list of only those individuals already included in the tree.

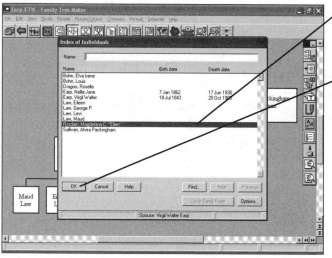

5. Click on the desired **individual** in the list. The selected individual will be highlighted.

6. Click on **OK**. The Index of Individuals dialog box will close.

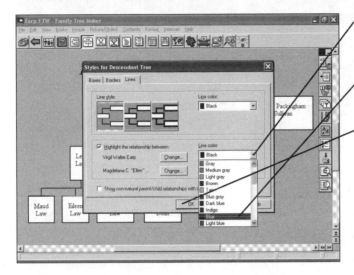

7. Click on the **Line color down arrow**. The Line color drop-down menu will appear.

8. Click on a **color**. The color will be selected.

9. Click on **OK**. The Styles dialog box will close and your changes will be saved.

Adding a Background Image

In working with your tree, there is nothing more interesting than enhancing its overall appearance. This can be done effectively by placing a picture in the background.

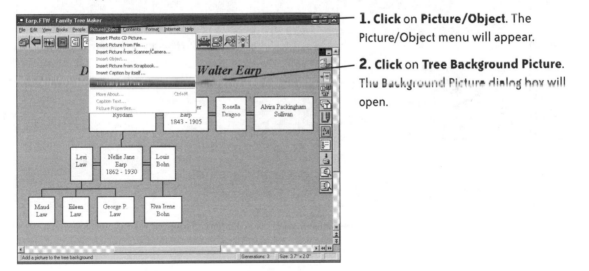

1. Click on **Picture/Object**. The Picture/Object menu will appear.

2. Click on **Tree Background Picture**. The Background Picture dialog box will open.

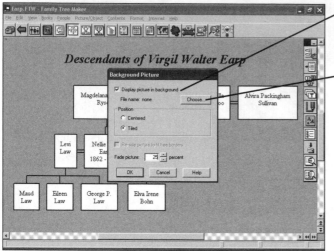

3. Click on the **Display picture in background check box**. The option will be selected.

4. Click on the **Choose button**. The Insert Picture window will open so you can select an image from a file.

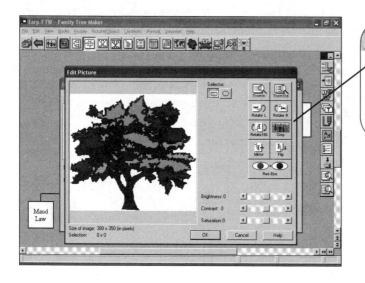

NOTE

At this point you can make changes to the selected picture. This is discussed in more detail in Chapter 17 "Creating a Scrapbook."

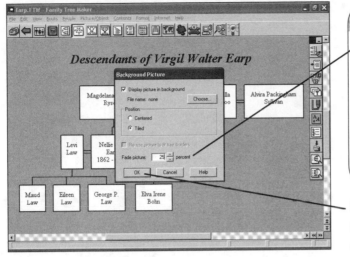

After selecting a digitized picture, you might want to fade the picture so that it does not make reading the tree difficult. The smaller the number in the Fade Picture field, the more faint the picture will appear behind the chart, making the chart easier to read.

5. Click on **OK**. The Background Picture dialog box will close and the picture will appear in the background of the report.

14

Working with Specialty Reports and the Research Journal

In addition to its many trees, Family Tree Maker also includes a number of other reports that allow you to understand what you have in your database and how the individuals might be related. In this chapter, you'll learn how to:

- Create a Custom Report
- Create a Kinship Report
- Create an Address Report
- Create a Birthday Report
- Use the Research Journal

Creating a Custom Report

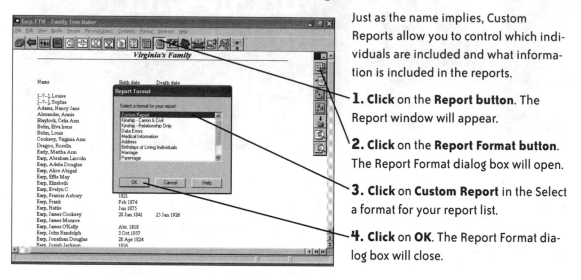

Just as the name implies, Custom Reports allow you to control which individuals are included and what information is included in the reports.

1. Click on the **Report button**. The Report window will appear.

2. Click on the **Report Format button**. The Report Format dialog box will open.

3. Click on **Custom Report** in the Select a format for your report list.

4. Click on **OK**. The Report Format dialog box will close.

Adding Items to Include in Your Report

The Custom Report might not have in it the information you want to include. However, this report is easy to adjust.

1. Click on the **Items to Include button**. The Items to Include in Report dialog box will open.

2. In the Available items list, **click** on an **item** that you want to include.

3. Click on the **Inclusion button**. The Options dialog box might open, depending on the item you've chosen to include.

> **NOTE**
>
> Not all of the Items to Include options will have detailed options. When nothing needs to be selected, the Options dialog box will not open.

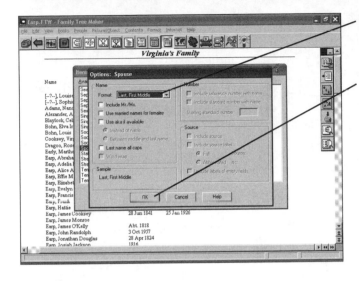

4. Select the desired **options**. A check mark will appear next to the options you have selected.

5. Click on **OK**. The Options dialog box will close and the items you selected will be included in the Each row of your report will contain list.

Choosing Individuals to Include in Your Report

You can limit the number of individuals appearing in the report if you do not want to show your entire database. You can do this individually or by relationship.

1. Click on the **Individuals to Include button**. The Include dialog box will open.

2. Click on the **Individuals to Include button**. The Individuals to Include dialog box will open.

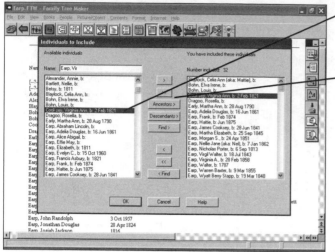

3. In the Available individuals list, **select** the **individual** you want to include.

4. Click on the appropriate **Inclusion button**. The individual you selected (and his or her ancestors or descendants, if applicable) will be moved to the You have included these individuals list.

NOTE

There are four major Inclusion buttons. The > button tells Family Tree Maker to include the single highlighted individual. The >> button will include all the individuals. The Ancestors button will include the ancestors of the highlighted individual. The Descendants button will include the descendants of the highlighted individual.

TIP

The Find button opens up the Find Individual dialog box which you were introduced to in Chapter 10 "Searching Your Family Tree File." You can search using name, date, location, source, and comment just as you can with the Find Individual option used in Chapter 10.

5. **Click** on **OK**. The Individuals to Include dialog box will close and your changes will be saved.

Using the Find Button to Remove Individuals

After you have created a list of individuals using the myriad searches available, you might discover that you want to remove selected individuals from the list, especially if you are trying to create a report of individuals from which to generate a new Family File or GEDCOM file.

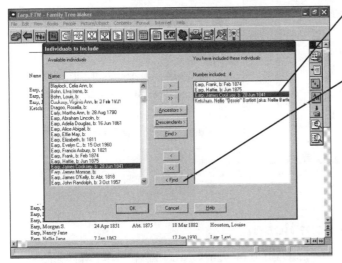

1. Click on an **individual** in the You have included these individuals list. The individual will be selected.

2. Click on the **<Find button**. The Remove Individuals dialog box will open.

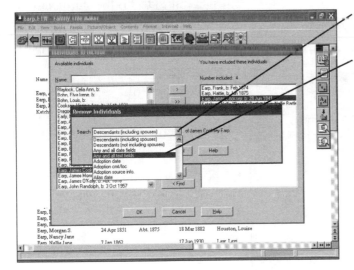

3. Click on the **Search down arrow**. The Search menu will appear.

4. Click on the desired **search option**. The option will be selected.

NOTE

You have the same search options in the Find and Remove (<Find) search as you had in the Find and Include (Find>) search. It just works in reverse, removing those individuals who fit the search criteria.

5. Press the **Tab key**. The cursor will move to the for field.

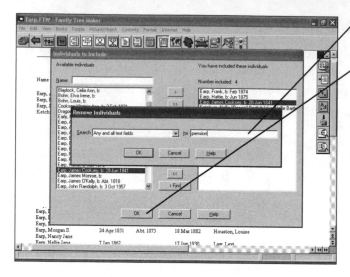

6. Type the **text, date, or name** for which you want to search.

7. Click on **OK**. The You have included these individuals list will be updated.

Formatting Your Custom Report

Once you have finally selected the individuals for your Custom Report, you will want to take as much care in the design of the report. You want to make sure it has enough information to easily identify the individuals included on the report.

1. Click on **Items to Include**. The Items to Include in Report dialog box will open.

2. Click on the **<< button**. The Each row of your report will contain list will be erased.

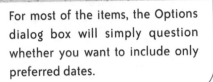

3. Click on an **item** in the Available items list. The item will be selected.

4. Click on the **Include button**. The Options dialog box will open.

NOTE

For most of the items, the Options dialog box will simply question whether you want to include only preferred dates.

5. Click on the **Format down arrow**. The Format menu will appear.

6. Click on the **appropriate format**. The format will be selected.

NOTE

As you make your choices, the sample in the lower-left corner of the dialog box will change.

7. Click on **OK**. The Options dialog box will close and the item will be listed in the Each row of your report will contain list.

TIP

Your report will probably need to contain the name of the individuals, at least one date (for identification purposes), and perhaps the name of the spouse (to make it easier to search for females during your research).

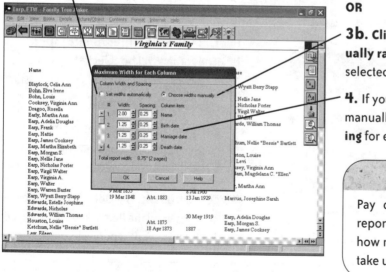

Adjusting Column Widths

Sometimes, in an effort to fit as much information in a report as possible, it is necessary to adjust the column widths.

1. Click on **Format**. The Format menu will appear.

2. Click on **Maximum Width for each Column**. The Maximum Width for Each Column dialog box will open.

3a. Click on the **Set widths automatically radio button**. The option will be selected.

OR

3b. Click on the **Choose widths manually radio button**. The option will be selected.

4. If you choose to adjust the widths manually, **adjust** the **width and spacing** for each column.

TIP

Pay close attention to the total report width. This lets you know how much space your columns will take up on the page.

5. **Click** on **OK**. The Maximum Width for Each Column dialog box will close.

Sorting Reports

One benefit of having your family history information in a database is that you have the ability to manipulate the data after it has been entered. You can sort the report based on the columns included.

1. Click on **Format**. The Format menu will appear.

2. Click on **Sort Report**. The Sort Report dialog box will open.

3. From the Sort by drop-down menu, **select** the **first column** by which you want to sort.

4a. Click on the **Ascending radio button** to sort in ascending order.

OR

4b. Click on the **Descending radio button** to sort in descending order.

5. From the Then by drop-down menu, **select** the **second column** by which you want to sort, if desired.

6. Click on **OK**. The Sort Report dialog box will close.

Exporting Reports to a Spreadsheet

There are times when you may want to not only sort your report, but also use it as a manner for tracking some of your research. You may want to create a listing of certain individuals to use as a starting point of a special project. Family Tree Maker lets you take the report you created and export it to a spreadsheet program.

1. Click on **File**. The File menu will appear.

2. Move the **mouse pointer** to the Export Report option. The Export Report submenu will appear.

3. Click on the **To Spreadsheet (CSV)** option. The Export Report dialog box will open.

4. Type in the **name** of the file.

5. Click on the **Save button**. The file will be saved and the Export Report dialog box will close.

NOTE

Remember to pay attention to where the file is being saved, so that you will be able to find it when you launch your spreadsheet program and go to open the file.

Creating a Kinship Report

Kinship Reports help you determine just how individuals in your database are related. The people making up several generations might be related in more than one way.

1. Click on **Format**. The Format menu will appear.

2. Click on **Report Format**. The Report Format dialog box will open.

3. Click on **Kinship - Relationship Only** in the Select a format for your report list. The Kinship - Relationship Only report will be selected.

4. Click on **OK**. The Report Format dialog box will close.

The following is a representation of the first screenshot showing the Kinship of Virgil Walter Earp report:

Name	Birth date	Relationship with Virgil Earp
[--?--], Louise		Mother-in-law
Adams, Nancy Jane		Half sister-in-law
Alexander, Annie		Wife of the father
Bartlett, Nellie		Sister-in-law
Betsy	1811	Aunt
Blaylock, Celia Ann		Sister-in-law
Bohn, Elva Irene		Granddaughter
Bohn, Louis		Son-in-law
Cooksey, Virginia Ann	2 Feb 1821	Mother
Dragoo, Rosella		Wife
Early, Martha Ann	28 Aug 1790	Grandmother
Earp, Abraham Lincoln		1st cousin
Earp, Adelia Douglas	16 Jun 1861	Sister
Earp, Alice Abigail		Half niece
Earp, Effie May		Half niece
Earp, Elizabeth	1811	Aunt
Earp, Evelyn C.	15 Oct 1960	1st cousin
Earp, Francis Asbury	1821	Uncle
Earp, Frank	Feb 1874	Nephew
Earp, Hattie	Jun 1875	Niece
Earp, James Cooksey	28 Jun 1841	Brother
Earp, James Monroe		1st cousin
Earp, James O'Kelly	Abt. 1818	Uncle

TIP

Remember that you can change the primary individual. Press F2 or click on the Index of Individuals button to open the Index of Individuals and select the person you want as the primary individual.

Working with Address and Birthday Reports

Whether you find yourself the keeper of addresses for the family association or you just want to print out a report of birthdays so you will be sure to send cards, Family Tree Maker has you covered.

Creating an Address Report

If you have taken advantage of the Address More About option for living individuals, you can print out a report with those addresses.

1. Open the **Report Format dialog box**, using one of the different methods you have learned earlier in this chapter.

2. Click on **Address** in the Select a format for your report list. The Address Report will be selected.

3. Click on **OK**. The Report Format dialog box will close.

TIP

You can determine which individuals are included in the Address Report. Simply click on the Individuals to Include button.

NOTE

You might have some unexpected individuals in your report. Individuals can "inherit" an address if one has been entered for a parent or spouse.

Creating the Birthday Report

Thanks to the Birthday Report, you no longer need to look through all the pages of your living family members to find birthdays. The Birthday Report can display the birthdays of all the living individuals in your database, or it can show just those you want to select.

1. Click on the **Report Format button**. The Report Format dialog box will open.

2. Select the **Birthdays of Living Individuals** report from the Select a format for your report list.

3. Click on **OK**.

The Report Format dialog box will close and the Birthday Report will be displayed.

Using the Research Journal

The Research Journal offers a means for tracking your past research and for making notes on future research.

1. Click on the **FamilyFinder Center button**. The FamilyFinder Center window will appear.

2. Click on **My Research Journal/To-Do List**. The Research Journal screen will appear.

Creating a New To-Do Item

The Research Journal allows you to record a list of items that still need to be accomplished in your research. By using the Research Journal, you no longer need to try to remember these items, Just simply look at your to-do list before your next research trip.

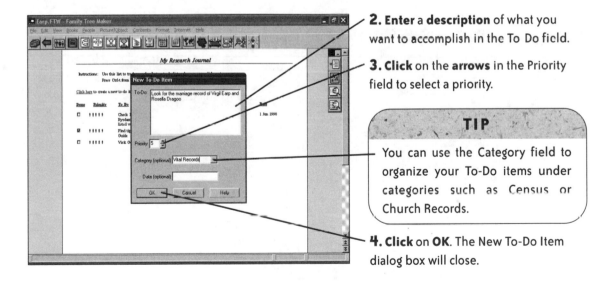

1. Click on the **Click here to create a new to-do item** link to add a To-Do item. The New To-Do Item dialog box will open.

2. Enter a **description** of what you want to accomplish in the To Do field.

3. Click on the **arrows** in the Priority field to select a priority.

TIP

You can use the Category field to organize your To-Do items under categories such as Census or Church Records.

4. Click on **OK**. The New To-Do Item dialog box will close.

Viewing Done or Not Done Items

The Research Journal is your road map of the research you have done and the research that still must be accomplished. There will be times when you will want to see it all, and other times when you will want to see only what you have done or what is left to do.

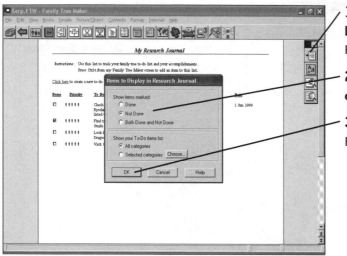

1. **Click** on the **Items to Display button**. The Items to Display in Research Journal dialog box will open.

2. **Select** a **Show items marked option**. The item will be selected.

3. **Click** on **OK**. The Items to Display in Research Journal dialog box will close.

The Research Journal will reflect the changes in the items listed based on whether the To-Do item has been done or is still pending.

Viewing Items for a Certain To-Do Category

Another way to affect the format of the Research Journal is through the To-Do categories. Usually based on resources or repositories, the To-Do categories allow you to narrow the focus of the report to just those entries for the selected category or categories.

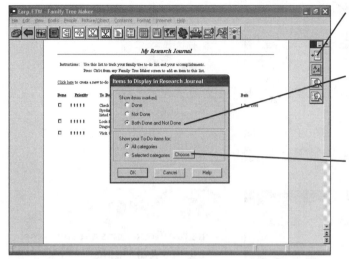

1. **Click** on the **Items to Display button**. The Items to Display in Research Journal dialog box will open.

2. **Click** on the **Both Done and Not Done option**. All items, whether done or not, will be included in the Research Journal.

3. **Click** on the **Choose button**. The Categories to Include dialog box will open. This dialog box is the same as many of the others you've seen. You simply select items from the Available list and place them in the other list.

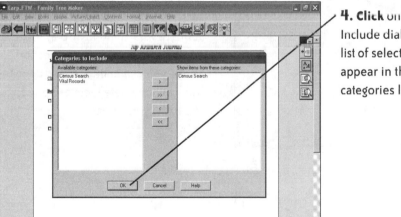

4. **Click** on **OK**. The Categories to Include dialog box will close, saving the list of selected categories as they appear in the Show items from these categories list.

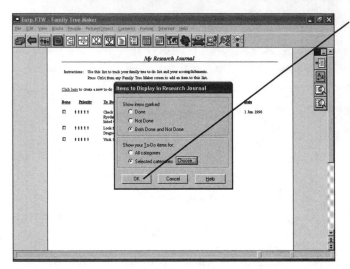

5. Click on **OK**. The Items to Display in Research Journal dialog box will close and the Research Journal will reflect your changes.

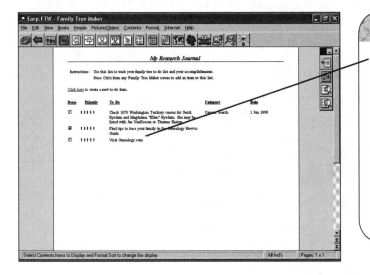

The two To-Do items already in the Research Journal (that refer to the Genealogy How-to Guide and Visit Genealogy.com) will appear regardless of the choices you make in terms of what items to display in the Show your To-Do items section. While you can mark them as Done, you cannot delete them as you can the items you enter.

If you want to delete a To-Do item that you have created, you can do so by clicking on the item so that it is highlighted and then pressing the Delete key.

Adding a To-Do Item Anytime

While the Research Journal report is useful, many Family Tree Maker users think they can only add new items by moving to the Research Journal section of the program. Actually, you can add a new to-do item any time you want. This feature is most useful when adding the new research.

1. Click on the **Family Page button**. The Family Page will appear.

2. Click on **Edit**. The Edit menu will appear.

3. Click on **Create New To Do Item**. The New To Do Item dialog box will open.

TIP

The Create New To Do Item option in the Edit menu also shows a hot key combination. Pressing the Control and the T key will also open the New To Do Item dialog box.

NOTE

You would fill out the fields in the New To Do Item dialog box as you learned earlier in this chapter. The next time you open the Research Journal the additional to-do items added this way will be listed.

15

Viewing and Printing Reports and Trees

Now that you have learned how to enter information and view some of the reports and trees, you're probably very interested in learning how to format them and print them out. In this chapter, you'll learn how to:

- View the tree you want to print
- Customize the view of the tree
- Change the print setup
- Print the tree
- Save the tree

Viewing the Tree You Want to Print

Family Tree Maker assumes that the tree or report you are interested in is the one on the screen, so you need to display the tree to print it.

1. Click on the **tree view** you want to print. A menu might appear, depending on which tree view you select.

2. If a menu does appear, **click** on the **tree type** you want to print. The tree will appear.

Customizing the View

After you have displayed the tree you want to print, you can fine-tune the text style, font, and size.

1. Click on the **Text Font, Style, & Size button**. The Text Font, Style, & Size dialog box will open.

> ### NOTE
>
> The complete name of the dialog box will depend on the tree or report that you have selected.

Changing the Text Font

One wonderful aspect of computers and modern printers is that you can be creative with the fonts you use. The fonts you can use can range from formal to fun.

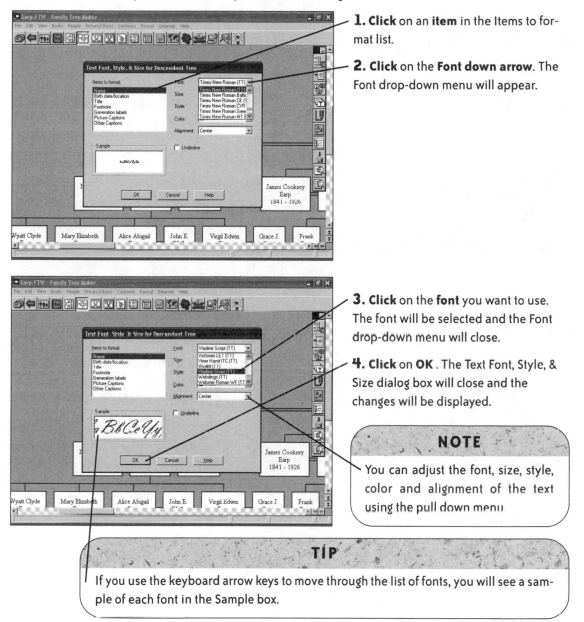

1. Click on an **item** in the Items to format list.

2. Click on the **Font down arrow**. The Font drop-down menu will appear.

3. Click on the **font** you want to use. The font will be selected and the Font drop-down menu will close.

4. Click on **OK**. The Text Font, Style, & Size dialog box will close and the changes will be displayed.

NOTE

You can adjust the font, size, style, color and alignment of the text using the pull down menu

TIP

If you use the keyboard arrow keys to move through the list of fonts, you will see a sample of each font in the Sample box.

Working with Borders

When sharing a tree with cousins or putting it into a book, you may want to customize the borders and background of the tree. Family Tree Maker offers a few border choices and the ability to change the color of the background of the tree.

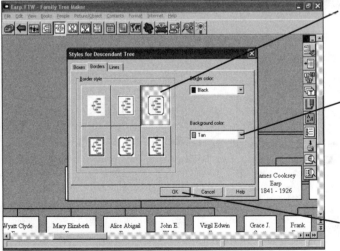

1. Click on the **Box, Line & Border Styles button**. The Styles for Tree dialog box will open.

2. Click on the **Borders Tab**. The borders options will be available.

3. Click on the desired **style**. The style will be selected.

NOTE

If you find when printing your trees or reports with a color printer that there is a background printing out, you can get rid of it by making sure the Background color option in the Borders section is set to none.

4. Click on **OK**. The Styles for Tree dialog box will close and the changes will be displayed.

Enhancing Your Tree with Templates

Another way to truly enhance your family tree chart is through the use of templates. Templates offer creative borders and other artwork to all of the individuals in the chart with just a simple selection.

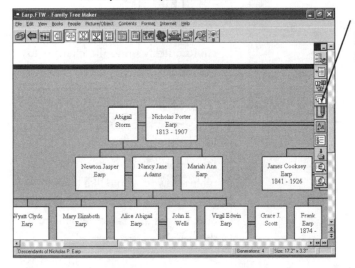

1. Click on the **Family Tree Templates button**. The Family Tree Templates dialog box will appear.

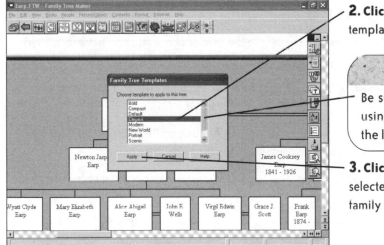

2. Click on the **template choice**. That template will be selected.

NOTE

Be sure to see all the templates by using the scroll bar on the right of the list.

3. Click on the **Apply push button**. The selected template will be applied to the family tree chart.

TIP

If you do not like the look of the template, and you have not done anything else, such as zooming in or out to view the template better, you can use the CTRL-Z keyboard shortcut to quickly undo the changes to the report.

NOTE

If you did make other changes to the report after applying the template and you would like to remove the template, simply follow the above steps and select Default from the template choices.

Printing the Tree

After you have made the necessary changes to the printer setup and you have formatted your tree the way you want, it is ready to print.

1. Click on **File**. The File menu will appear.

2. Click on **Print Tree**. The Print Tree dialog box will open.

NOTE

The actual name of the Print Tree dialog box will vary depending on the report selected.

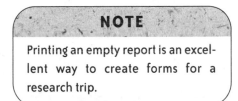

3. In the Copies field, **enter** the **number of copies** you want to print.

4. Select the **Print empty check box** to print an empty report.

5. Select the **Print color check box** to print the report in color, if you have a color printer.

> **NOTE**
>
> Printing an empty report is an excellent way to create forms for a research trip.

6a. Click on **OK**. The report will be sent to the printer.

OR

6b. Click on **Cancel**. The report will not be printed.

Saving the Tree in PDF Format

Many of us would like to save the trees in a format that we can share either on disk or through e-mail with those with whom we are corresponding. Due to the nature of the formatting of these trees, this is done best using the PDF format, the Portable Document Format created by Adobe.

1. Click on the **File menu**. The File menu will appear.

2. Move the **mouse** pointer to Export Tree. The Export tree submenu will appear.

3. Click on **To Acrobat (PDF)**. The Export Tree dialog box will open.

4. Type in the **name of the file** in the **File name field**.

5. Click the **Save button**. The file will be saved.

NOTE

The Save as type option will default to PDF. Remember that when sharing this with others they must have the Adobe Acrobat Reader installed on their system to read the file.

16

Creating Genealogy Style and Genealogical Source Reports

After you have entered all your information, you will want to share it with family members and other researchers. The Genealogy Style Reports are one of the best ways to do this. In this chapter, you'll learn how to:

- Select a genealogy style

- Include sources as endnotes in reports

- Format the report

- Locate conflicting data

- Create a Bibliography Report

- Create a Documented Events Report

Using Genealogy Style Reports

Genealogy Reports in Family Tree Maker are narrative reports containing genealogical information, basic facts, and biographical details. These are the most common formats you see in published family histories.

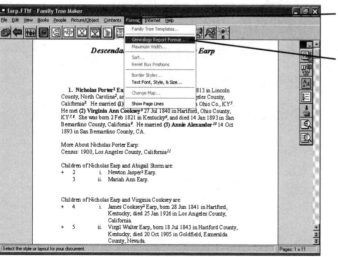

Working with Register Format

The Register format gets its name from the journal that devised it, *The New England Historic Genealogical Register*. This report lists individuals in order of descendants.

1. Click on the **Genealogy Report button**. The Genealogy Report will appear.

2. Click on **Format**. The Format menu will appear.

3. Click on **Genealogy Report Format**. The Genealogy Report Format dialog box will open.

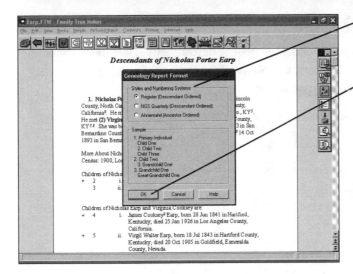

4. Click on the **Register (Descendant Ordered) radio button**. The option will be selected.

5. Click on **OK**. The Genealogy Report Format dialog box will close.

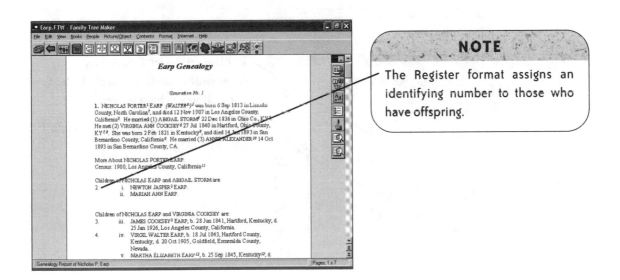

NOTE

The Register format assigns an identifying number to those who have offspring.

Working with **NGSQ** Format

The NGSQ format also displays individuals in order of descendants. It was named after the *National Genealogical Society Quarterly*, the journal of the National Genealogical Society.

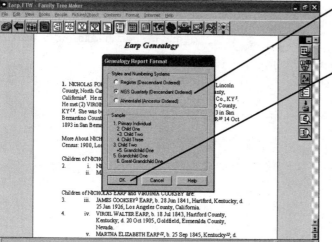

1. Click on the **Format button**. The Genealogy Report Format dialog box will open.

2. Click on the **NGS Quarterly (Descendant Ordered) radio button**. The option will be selected.

3. Click on **OK**. The Genealogy Report Format dialog box will close.

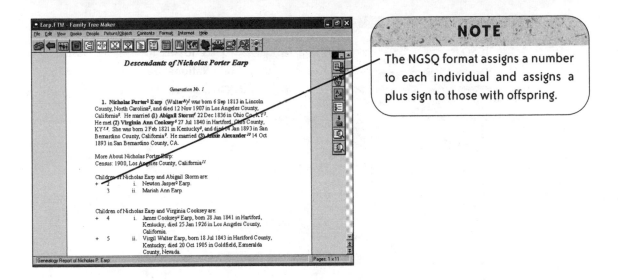

NOTE

The NGSQ format assigns a number to each individual and assigns a plus sign to those with offspring.

Using the Ahnentafel Report

Ahnentafel is a German word that means "ancestor table" or "family table." This report lists individuals in an ancestral order. This is the opposite of the other two reports.

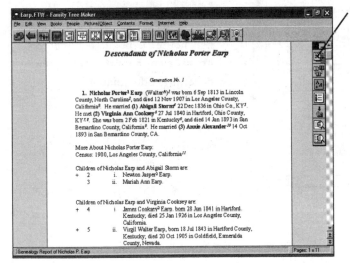

1. Click on the **Format button**. The Genealogy Report Format dialog box will open.

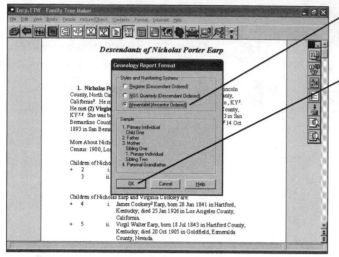

2. Click on the **Ahnentafel (Ancestor Ordered) radio button**. The option will be selected.

3. Click on **OK**. The Genealogy Report Format dialog box will close.

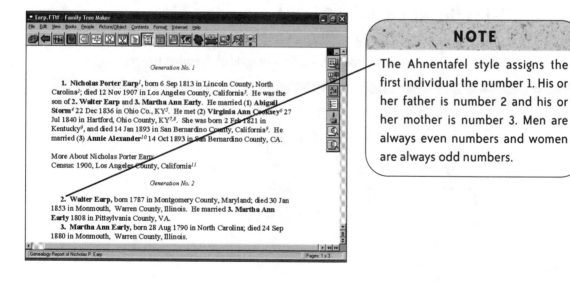

NOTE

The Ahnentafel style assigns the first individual the number 1. His or her father is number 2 and his or her mother is number 3. Men are always even numbers and women are always odd numbers.

Using Endnotes

Genealogy Style Reports include source citations. These can be included in the body of the report or they can be printed as endnotes.

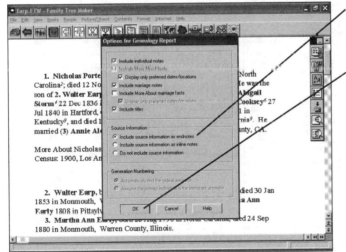

1. Click on the **Options button**. The Options for Genealogy Report dialog box will open.

2. Click on the **Include source information as endnotes radio button**. The option will be selected.

3. Click on OK. The Options for Genealogy Report dialog box will close.

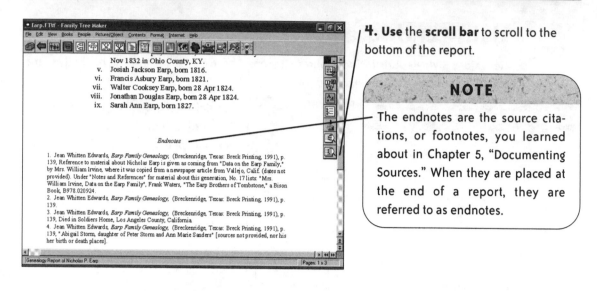

4. Use the **scroll bar** to scroll to the bottom of the report.

NOTE

The endnotes are the source citations, or footnotes, you learned about in Chapter 5, "Documenting Sources." When they are placed at the end of a report, they are referred to as endnotes.

Formatting the Report

In addition to the different styles of reports, there are other items that need to be considered, such as page numbering and the type of notes to include.

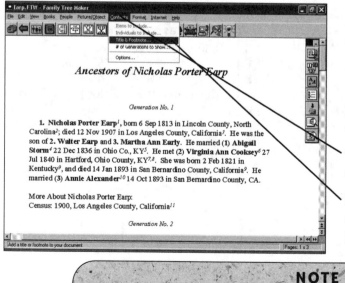

Adjusting Title and Page Numbering

Family Tree Maker has default settings for the title and page number, but you can change these settings.

1. Click on **Contents**. The Contents menu will appear.

2. Click on **Title & Footnote**. The Title & Footnote for Genealogy Report dialog box will open.

NOTE

All of the reports allow for title and footnote options. The title of this dialog box will vary depending on which type of report or tree you are using.

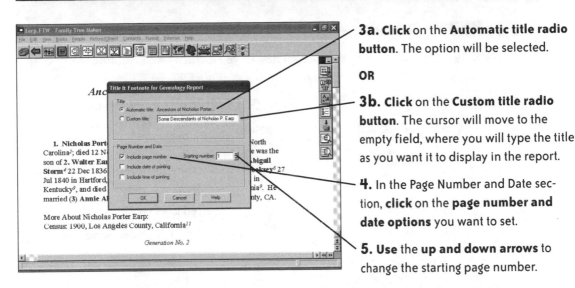

3a. Click on the **Automatic title radio button**. The option will be selected.

OR

3b. Click on the **Custom title radio button**. The cursor will move to the empty field, where you will type the title as you want it to display in the report.

4. In the Page Number and Date section, **click** on the **page number and date options** you want to set.

5. Use the **up and down arrows** to change the starting page number.

6. Click on **OK**. The Title & Footnote for Genealogy Report dialog box will close.

Changing the Number of Generations

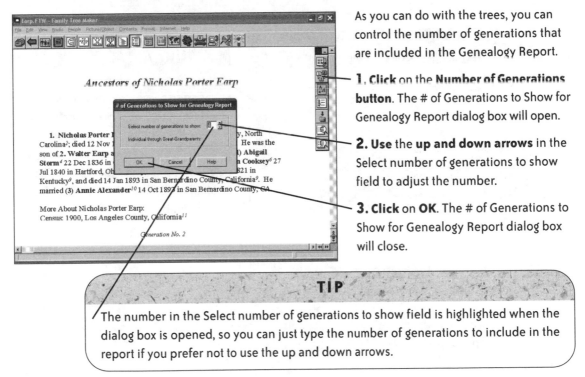

As you can do with the trees, you can control the number of generations that are included in the Genealogy Report.

1. Click on the **Number of Generations button**. The # of Generations to Show for Genealogy Report dialog box will open.

2. Use the **up and down arrows** in the Select number of generations to show field to adjust the number.

3. Click on **OK**. The # of Generations to Show for Genealogy Report dialog box will close.

TIP

The number in the Select number of generations to show field is highlighted when the dialog box is opened, so you can just type the number of generations to include in the report if you prefer not to use the up and down arrows.

Including Notes and Other Options

In Chapter 7, "Understanding More About Notes," you learned how to include family stories in your family file. These stories can be included in printed reports.

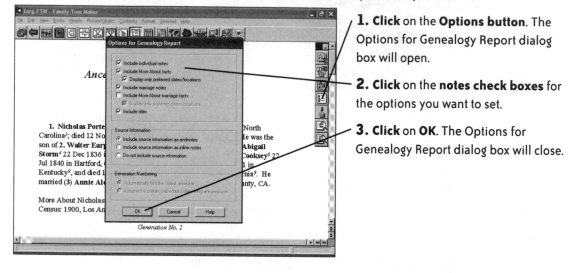

1. Click on the **Options button**. The Options for Genealogy Report dialog box will open.

2. Click on the **notes check boxes** for the options you want to set.

3. Click on **OK**. The Options for Genealogy Report dialog box will close.

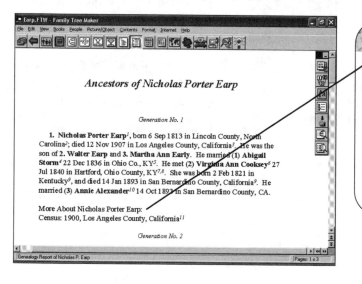

TIP

It is a good idea to read through the report to see if the notes are appropriate and should be included. Even if you have not opened the Options dialog box, some notes will be included because Family Tree Maker has note options turned on by default.

Locating Conflicting Facts

Family Tree Maker allows you to enter duplicate facts. This is by design, because you will find dates in your research that conflict with each other and you want to record each of them. Family Tree Maker also lets you conduct a search based on these conflicting facts.

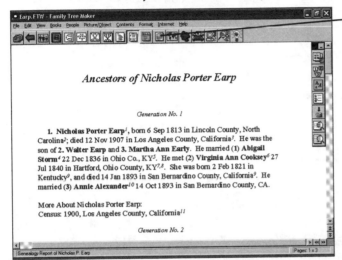

1. Click on the **Report button**. The last report opened will appear.

2. Click on the **Format button**. The Report Format dialog box will open.

3. Scroll down until you reach the bottom of the Select a format for your report list.

4. Click on **Alternate Facts**. The option will be selected.

5. Click on **OK**. The Report Format dialog box will close.

6. Click on an **individual** or **fact** from the report. The individual or fact will be selected.

7. Click on **View**. The View menu will appear.

8. Move the **mouse pointer** to More About. The More About menu will appear.

9. Click on **Facts**. The More About Facts window will appear.

NOTE

You can now view the facts for the individual.

Creating a Bibliography Report

A bibliography is a list of books and sources. These are the sources you have used to compile your Family Tree file. A Bibliography Report is a useful reference tool.

1. Click on the **Report button**. The Report will appear.

2. Click on the **Format button**. The Report Format dialog box will open.

3. Click on **Bibliography** in the Select a format for your report list. The option will be selected.

4. Click on **OK**. The Report Format dialog box will close.

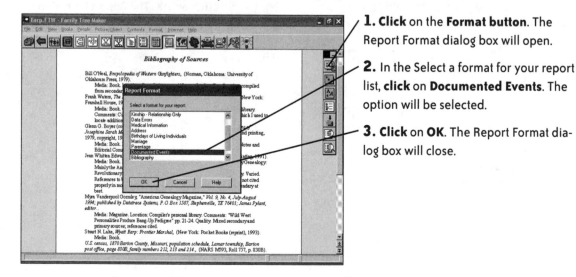

5. Click on the **Options button**. The Options for Bibliography Report dialog box will open.

6a. Click on **Standard Bibliography** to create a standard bibliography.

OR

6b. Click on **Annotated Bibliography** to create an annotated bibliography.

NOTE

The annotated bibliography includes the full source citation and comments by the researcher about the source.

Creating a Documented Events Report

Understanding how you came to the conclusions you did in your Family Tree file is usually directly related to the sources used. The Documented Events Report is a clear list of the individuals and events you have documented.

1. Click on the **Format button**. The Report Format dialog box will open.

2. In the Select a format for your report list, **click** on **Documented Events**. The option will be selected.

3. Click on **OK**. The Report Format dialog box will close.

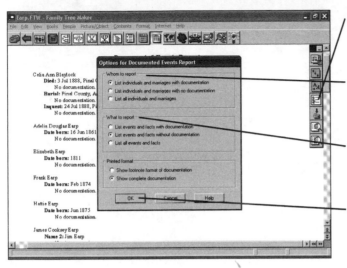

4. Click on the **Options button**. The Options for Documented Events Report dialog box will open.

5. Click on the desired **Whom to report radio button**. The option will be selected.

6. Click on the desired **What to report radio button**. The option will be selected.

7. Click on **OK**. The Options for Documented Events Report dialog box will close.

PART V

Publishing Your Family History

Chapter 17
Creating a Scrapbook 263

Chapter 18
Creating a Family History
Book 285

Chapter 19
Creating Your Personal FTM
Homepage 303

17 Creating a Scrapbook

Using present technology, it is possible to create beautiful reports and enhance them by adding digital photographs. Family Tree Maker calls these reports scrapbooks. In this chapter, you'll learn how to:

- Use a scrapbook

- Insert images into a scrapbook

- Enter information about scrapbook items

- Rearrange scrapbook objects

- Edit pictures or objects

- Search for objects

- Share your scrapbook

Using the Scrapbook

The scrapbook is where you can work with digitized files such as scanned photographs. There are scrapbooks for individuals and for marriages.

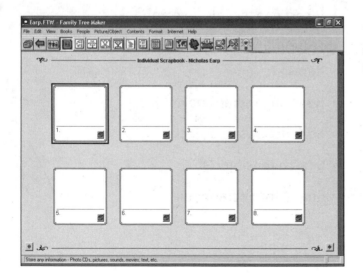

1. Click on the **Family Page button**. The Family Page window will appear.

2. Click on the **Scrapbk button**.

The Individual Scrapbook window will appear. Each frame can hold a digitized image, a sound clip, or another object.

Inserting Scrapbook Objects

While most of the items you will work with will be scanned photographs, Family Tree Maker does support sound clips and OLE (*Object Linking and Embedding*) objects.

Using Graphics Images

Scanning photographs helps to preserve them, and they can then be included in the reports you print from Family Tree Maker. But first you need to import the graphics image files.

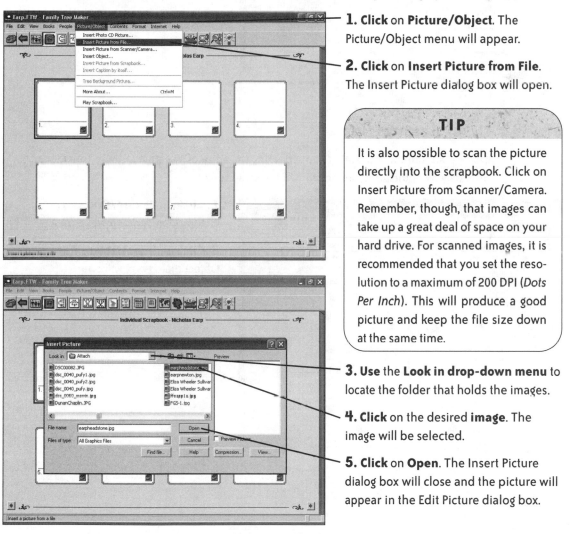

1. Click on **Picture/Object**. The Picture/Object menu will appear.

2. Click on **Insert Picture from File**. The Insert Picture dialog box will open.

TIP

It is also possible to scan the picture directly into the scrapbook. Click on Insert Picture from Scanner/Camera. Remember, though, that images can take up a great deal of space on your hard drive. For scanned images, it is recommended that you set the resolution to a maximum of 200 DPI (*Dots Per Inch*). This will produce a good picture and keep the file size down at the same time.

3. Use the **Look in drop-down menu** to locate the folder that holds the images.

4. Click on the desired **image**. The image will be selected.

5. Click on **Open**. The Insert Picture dialog box will close and the picture will appear in the Edit Picture dialog box.

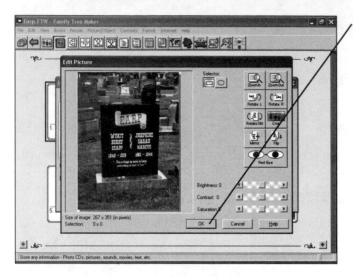

6. Click on **OK**. The Edit Picture dialog box will close.

Using Sound Clips

There is something fascinating about hearing the voice of a relative. Family Tree Maker offers a way of including sound clips in the scrapbook.

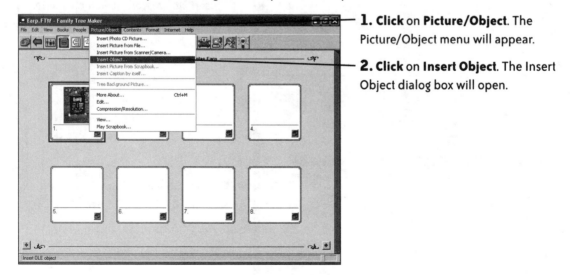

1. Click on **Picture/Object**. The Picture/Object menu will appear.

2. Click on **Insert Object**. The Insert Object dialog box will open.

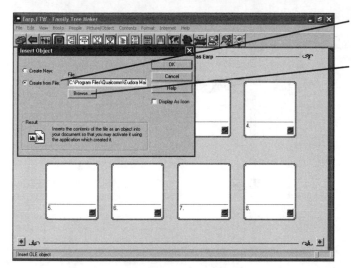

3. Click on the **Create from File radio button**. The option will be selected.

4. Click on the **Browse button**. The Browse dialog box will open.

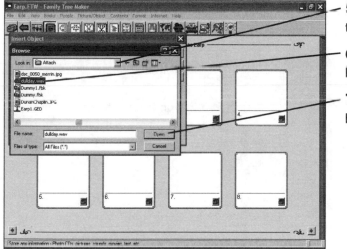

5. Use the **Look in drop-down menu** to locate the proper folder.

6. Click on the desired **file**. The file will be selected.

7. Click on **Open**. The Browse dialog box will close.

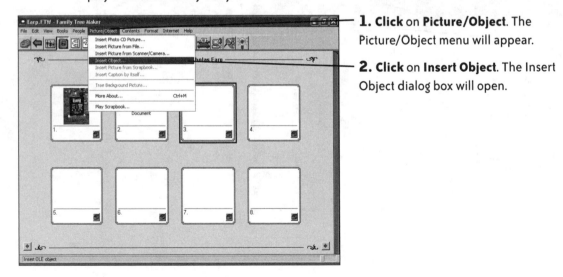

8. Click on the **Display As Icon check box**. The option will be selected.

9. Click on **OK**. The Insert Object dialog box will close.

Using OLE Objects

Object Linking and Embedding (OLE) allows you to launch another program from within Family Tree Maker. You might want to do this so you can open a word-processing file to display a detailed family story.

1. Click on **Picture/Object**. The Picture/Object menu will appear.

2. Click on **Insert Object**. The Insert Object dialog box will open.

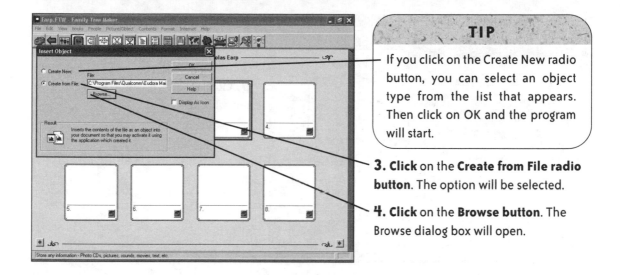

TIP

If you click on the Create New radio button, you can select an object type from the list that appears. Then click on OK and the program will start.

3. Click on the **Create from File radio button**. The option will be selected.

4. Click on the **Browse button**. The Browse dialog box will open.

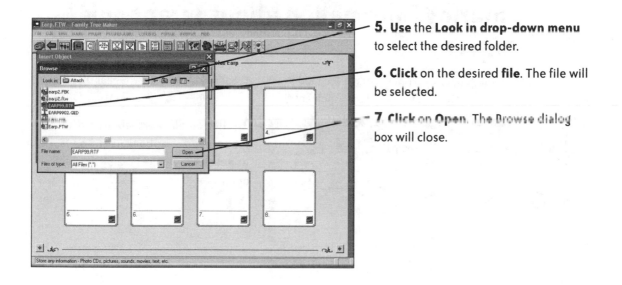

5. Use the **Look in drop-down menu** to select the desired folder.

6. Click on the desired **file**. The file will be selected.

7. Click on **Open**. The Browse dialog box will close.

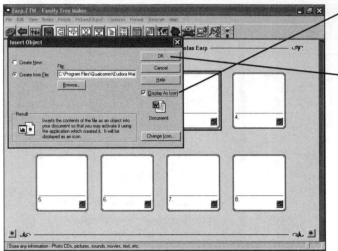

8. Click on the **Display As Icon check box**. Family Tree Maker will insert an icon in the scrapbook.

9. Click on **OK**. The Insert Object dialog box will close.

Entering Information about Scrapbook Objects

To help you know what you have selected in your scrapbook, Family Tree Maker offers a More About screen for each scrapbook entry.

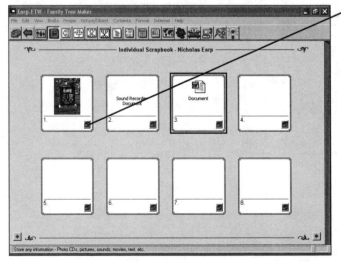

1. Click on the **More About button** for the selected scrapbook item. The More About Picture/Object dialog box will open.

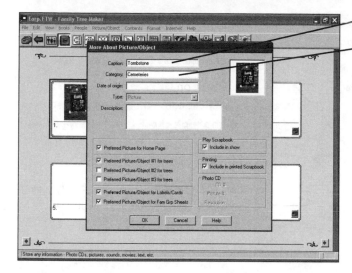

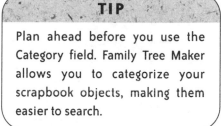

2. Type a **caption** in the Caption field.

3. Type a **category** in the Category field.

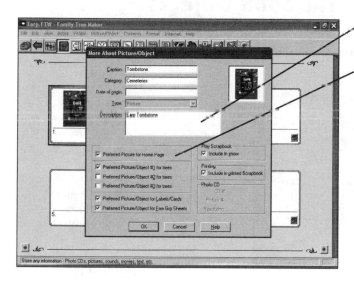

4. Type a **description** for the object in the Description field.

5. Select the desired **preferred check box(es)**. The option(s) will be selected.

6. Click on the **Include in show check box** if you want the object to display when you play the scrapbook as a slideshow.

7. Click on the **Include in printed Scrapbook check box** if you want the object to display in the printed scrapbook.

8. Click on **OK**. The More About Picture/Object dialog box will close.

Rearranging Scrapbook Objects

There might be a time when you want the items or objects in the scrapbook to display in a particular order that's different from the way you originally entered them.

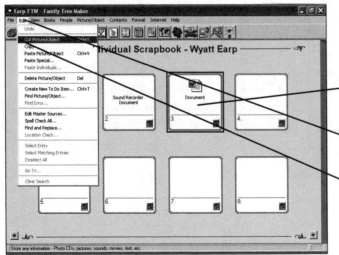

Moving Objects

One way to rearrange the objects inserted in a scrapbook is to move them.

1. Click on the **object** you want to move. The object will be selected.

2. Click on **Edit**. The Edit menu will appear.

3. Click on **Cut Picture/Object**. The picture will be moved to the Clipboard.

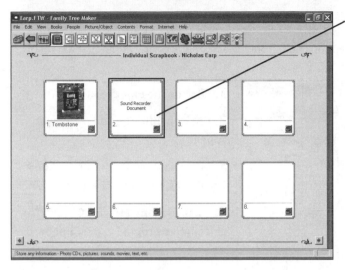

4. Click in the **frame** where you want to place the object.

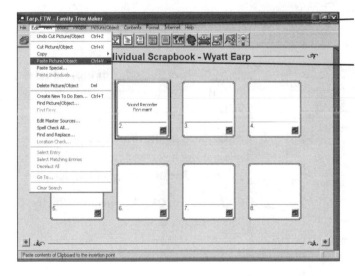

5. Click on **Edit**. The Edit menu will appear.

6. Click on **Paste Picture/Object**. The object will be pasted in the new position.

Copying Objects

You can copy and paste a scrapbook item from the scrapbook of one individual to that of another.

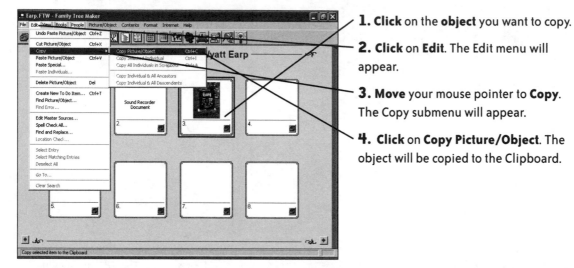

1. Click on the **object** you want to copy.

2. Click on **Edit**. The Edit menu will appear.

3. Move your mouse pointer to **Copy**. The Copy submenu will appear.

4. Click on **Copy Picture/Object**. The object will be copied to the Clipboard.

5. Click on the **Index of Individuals button**. The Index of Individuals dialog box will open.

6. Click on the **individual** into whose scrapbook you want to paste the object. The individual will be selected.

7. Click on **OK**. The new individual's scrapbook will open.

8. Click on the **frame** where you want to place the object.

9. Click on **Edit**. The Edit menu will appear.

10. Click on **Paste Picture/Object**. The copied object will be placed in the scrapbook.

Enhancing Your Images

Family Tree Maker has included the ability to rotate, crop, mirror, and flip images. You can also adjust color and brightness and remove red eye from the digitized photos.

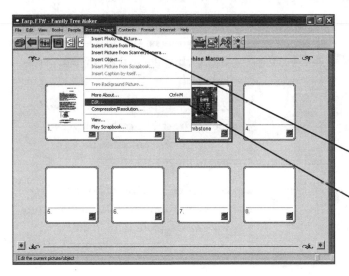

Cropping an Image

There are times when the scanned image shows more than you wish to include in your reports. By cropping the image, you can limit the part of the picture that will be used in your scrapbook.

1. Click on **Picture/Object**. The Picture/Object menu will appear.

2. Click on **Edit**. The Edit Picture dialog box will open.

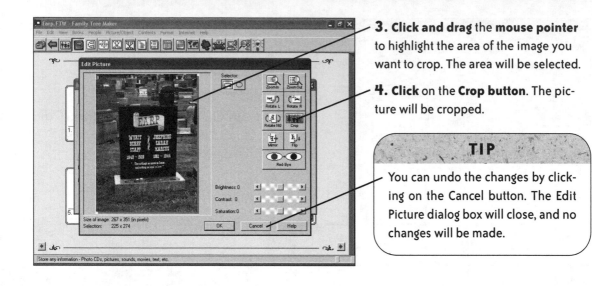

3. Click and drag the **mouse pointer** to highlight the area of the image you want to crop. The area will be selected.

4. Click on the **Crop button**. The picture will be cropped.

TIP

You can undo the changes by clicking on the Cancel button. The Edit Picture dialog box will close, and no changes will be made.

Adjusting Color and Brightness

There are times when the image has shadows or the image is not as clear as you had hoped. Through adjusting the color, brightness and saturation, it may be possible to better see the individuals in the picture, bringing them somewhat out of the shadow.

1. Click on the **right** or **left arrow** for the **brightness**. The brightness level will change, brighter to the right and darker to the left.

2. Click on the **right** or **left arrow** for the **contrast**. The contrast level will change, more contrast to the right and less to the left.

3. Click on the **right** or **left arrow** for the **saturation**. The color of the picture will change, more color to the right, more like a black and white picture to the left.

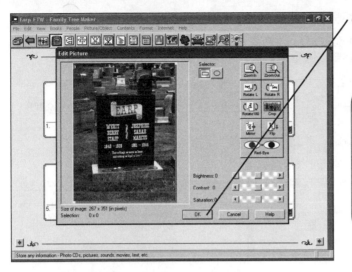

4. Click on **OK**. The changes will be made to the image and the Edit Picture dialog box will close.

> **TIP**
>
> To make dramatic changes to the brightness, contrast, or saturation, use the scroll bar that is located between the buttons for each. You drag to the right to increase or to the left to decrease.

Correcting Red Eye

There are times when the eyes in family photos look red or hollow. This has long been a frustration of color photos and is now fixable when using the scanned images in your scrapbook. Be sure you have opened one of the pictures you want to change.

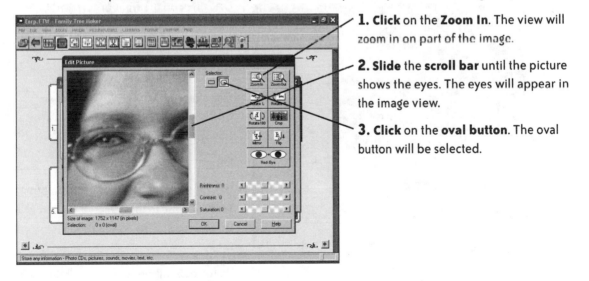

1. Click on the **Zoom In**. The view will zoom in on part of the image.

2. Slide the **scroll bar** until the picture shows the eyes. The eyes will appear in the image view.

3. Click on the **oval button**. The oval button will be selected.

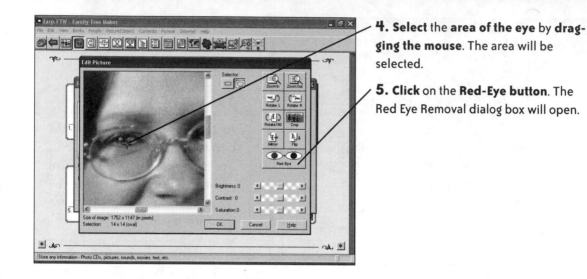

4. Select the **area of the eye** by **dragging the mouse**. The area will be selected.

5. Click on the **Red-Eye button**. The Red Eye Removal dialog box will open.

TIP

Generally you will not need to do anything at this point other than to click the OK push button. The red eye removal is automatic. If you do not like the results, you can manually adjust the colors.

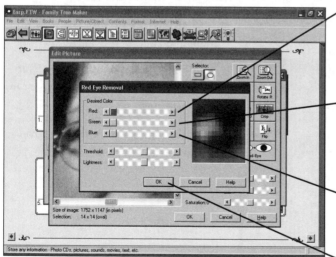

6a. Click on the **right** or **left Red button**. The red in the selected section will be adjusted.

OR

6b. Click on the **right** or **left Green button**. The green in the selected section will be adjusted.

OR

6c. Click on the **right** or **left Blue button**. The blue in the selected section will be adjusted.

7. Click on **OK**. The Red Eye Removal dialog box will close and the picture will reflect the changes made.

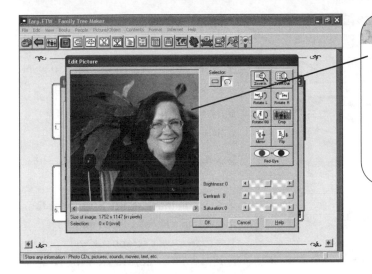

NOTE

Be sure to examine the changes to the image by using the Zoom Out to view the picture in its entirety. If you do not like the changes, simply click the Cancel button to close the Edit Picture dialog box and then begin again.

Searching for Objects

While it may not seem possible now, the more items you add, the quicker you will need to rely on the abilities of the Find features to locate specific scrapbook objects.

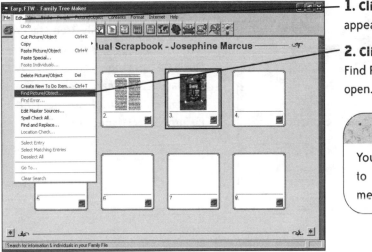

1. Click on **Edit**. The Edit menu will appear.

2. Click on **Find Picture/Object**. The Find Picture/Object dialog box will open.

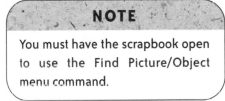

NOTE

You must have the scrapbook open to use the Find Picture/Object menu command.

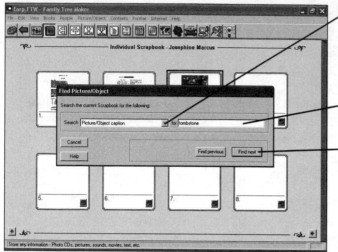

3. Click on the **Search down arrow**. The Search drop-down menu will appear.

4. Click on the **search option** you want to use. The option will be selected.

5. In the for field, **type** the **term** for which you want to search.

6. Click on the **Find next button**. The Family Page window will appear.

7. Click on the **Scrapbk button** for the individual who is in the Family Page. The individual's scrapbook will appear, and you will be able to view the scrapbook objects, one of which will fit your search criteria.

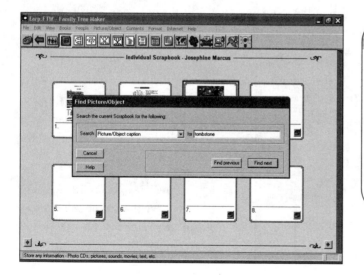

NOTE

Continue to click on the Find next button until the Family Tree Maker has found the object you want. Once that person's Family Page is displayed, you can click on the Cancel button to close the Find Picture/Object dialog box.

Sharing Your Scrapbook

When you have put together the digitized images with, say, the digitized interview of your relative, you may want to share it with others.

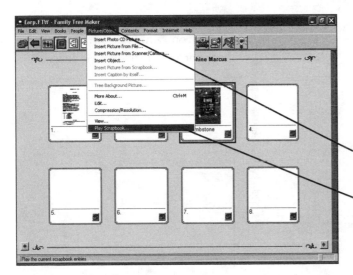

Playing a Scrapbook

Family reunions are a great place to share scrapbooks. Using Family Tree Maker, all your research and scrapbooks can be shown very effectively on a computer with speakers.

1. Click on **Picture/Object**. The Picture/Object menu will appear.

2. Click on **Play Scrapbook**. The Play Scrapbook dialog box will open.

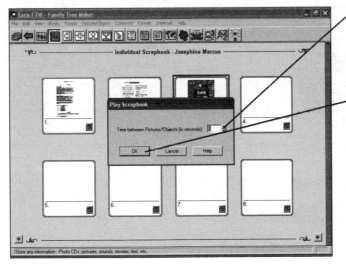

3. Use the **up and down arrows** in the Time between Pictures/Objects (in seconds) field to adjust the delay between objects.

4. Click on **OK**. The scrapbook will be played.

TIP

A sound file cannot play at the same time a slide is being viewed. If you have combined the two, you will find that you have a blank screen while the sound file runs its course.

Printing a Scrapbook

Most of the time, you will share your scrapbook by printing it out. Remember, the printed scrapbook includes only digitized images.

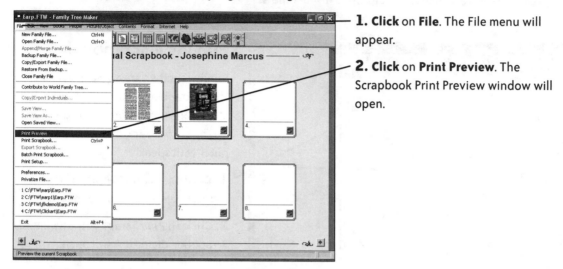

1. Click on **File**. The File menu will appear.

2. Click on **Print Preview**. The Scrapbook Print Preview window will open.

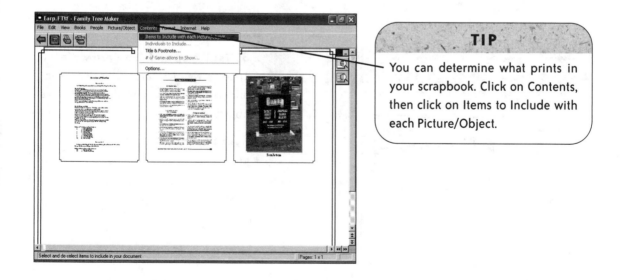

TIP

You can determine what prints in your scrapbook. Click on Contents, then click on Items to Include with each Picture/Object.

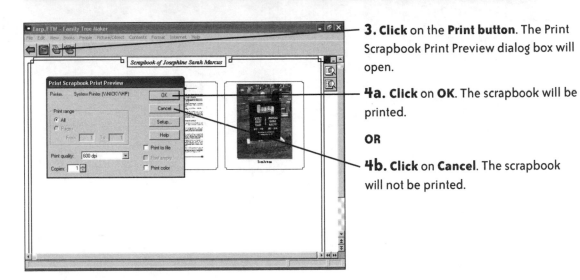

3. Click on the **Print button**. The Print Scrapbook Print Preview dialog box will open.

4a. Click on **OK**. The scrapbook will be printed.

OR

4b. Click on **Cancel**. The scrapbook will not be printed.

18

Creating a Family History Book

For many researchers, the ultimate goal is to publish a record of their ancestry. Family Tree Maker has long offered one of the easiest ways to put a variety of reports together to share with family, friends, or colleagues. In this chapter, you'll learn how to:

- Select specific reports and trees
- Organize selected items
- Work with images
- Add page breaks
- Create a customized index

Selecting Available Items

You have looked at many of the trees and reports that Family Tree Maker can create, but you might have been unaware that you can select these and put them together to create a book. One of the first things you have to do is decide what items to select. Following is a list of possible items to include in the book, from the title page to the index, including many family trees and narrative reports.

- Front Matter (title page, copyright notice, and so on)
- Introduction
- Ancestor Trees
- Descendant Trees
- Hourglass Trees
- Kinship Reports
- Narrative Reports
- Timelines
- Calendars
- Bibliography
- Index

1. Click on the **Publishing Center button**. The Publishing Center will appear.

2. Click on **Create a Family Book**. The New Book dialog box will open.

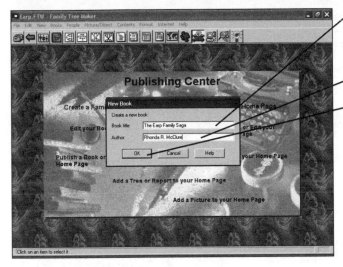

3. Type the **book title** in the Book title field and **press** the **Tab key**. The cursor will move to the Author field.

4. Type the **author's name**.

5. Click on **OK**. The Books window will appear.

Selecting Front Matter

When you open any book, the first pages you look at contain what Family Tree Maker refers to as the front matter. The title page, copyright notice, dedication, and table of contents are such items. When you first create your book, you will need to decide which of these you want to include.

1. In the Available items list, **double-click** on **Text Item**. The Add text item dialog box will open.

2. Click on the desired **text item**. The item will be selected.

3. Click on **OK**. The selected text item will be added to the Outline for list.

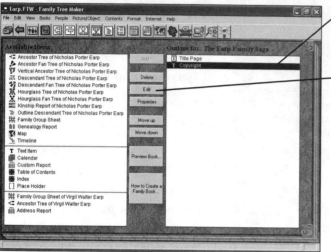

4. In the Outline for list, **click** on the newly added **text item**. The option buttons will be activated.

5. Click on **Edit**. The text editor window will open and display the selected item.

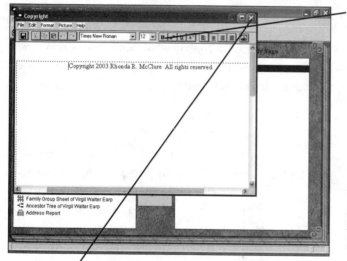

6. Use the **toolbar buttons** to make changes to the item.

> **TIP**
>
> The text editor works much like any other word-processing program. If you click on one of the toolbar buttons, such as italics, before you type, then the text you enter will be in italics. To change something that has already been written, you must highlight the text before choosing one of the toolbar options.

7. Click on the **Close button**. You will be prompted to save the book item; click on OK.

> **NOTE**
>
> You are not limited to a single text item. You might want to repeat steps 1 through 6 to add additional items such as a copyright notice, a dedication, and an introduction.

Adding Trees and Reports

A book of your ancestors should contain a number of different trees and reports. It is important to keep your audience in mind when you're deciding what to include. You can create different books for different groups of individuals, so that the one you share with your family is more personal and less formal than the one you share with another genealogist.

1. Click on the **tree or report** you want to include. The tree or report will be highlighted.

2. Click on **Add**. The tree or report will be added to the Outline for list.

> **TIP**
>
> You can select any of the reports, trees, or other options in the Available items list. You will learn to organize them later in this chapter, in the "Organizing the Items" section.

3. Double-click on **Genealogy Report**. The Add Genealogy Report dialog box will open.

4. Select the **type of Genealogy Report** to add. The option will be selected.

5. Click on **OK**. The Add Genealogy Report dialog box will close and the Genealogy Report will appear in the Outline for list.

Including Text with Pictures

Most of your family will want to see pictures in the book you share with them. While you can include them in some of the trees and reports, there are other times when you might want to have more control over the image. You can take this control by adding a Text Item with Pictures.

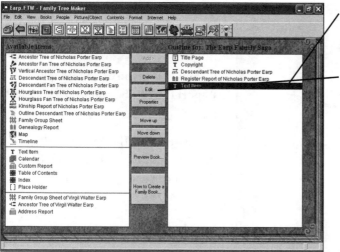

1. In the Available Items list, **double-click** on **Text Item**. The Add text item dialog box will open.

2. Select the desired **text item**.

3. Click on **OK**. The Add text item dialog box will close.

4. In the Outline for list, **click** on the newly added **text item**. Additional option buttons will be activated.

5. Click on **Edit**. The Text Item edit window will open.

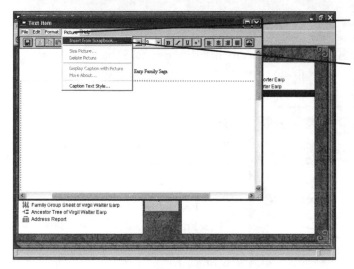

6. Click on **Picture**. The Picture menu will appear.

7. Click on **Insert from Scrapbook**. The Individuals with Scrapbook Pictures dialog box will open.

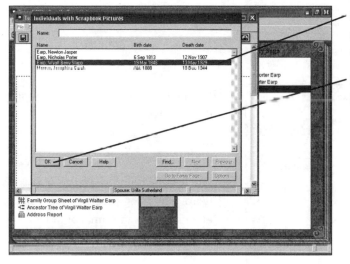

8. Click on the **individual** whose scrapbook you want to access. The individual will be highlighted.

9. Click on **OK**. The Insert Scrapbook Picture dialog box will open.

NOTE

If the displayed individual's scrapbook does not include the picture you were expecting, you can click on Select new individual and the Individuals with Scrapbook Pictures dialog box will open again.

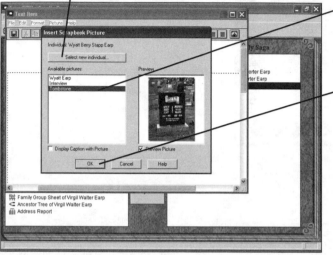

10. Click on the **picture** you want to include. The picture will be displayed in the Preview box, if you have the Preview Picture check box selected.

11. Click on **OK**. The Insert Scrapbook Picture dialog box will close and the picture will be included in the Text Item window.

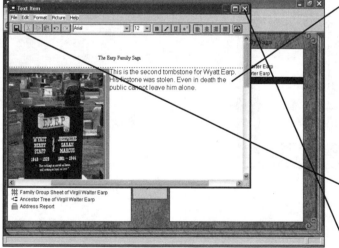

12. Type the **text** you want to associate with the image.

TIP

The Text Item window is similar to a word-processing program. You can alter the font and format of the text and the image within that window.

13. Click on the **Save button**. The changes to the text item will be saved.

14. Click on the **Close button**. The Text Item window will close.

Working with Outline Items

After you have decided which reports and trees you want to include in your book, you can begin to organize their order in the Outline for list. This is the order in which they will print when you send your book to the printer. You can also control which of your reports will start a new chapter in the book.

Organizing the Items

When you added to the Outline for list, Family Tree Maker simply placed the newly added tree or report at the bottom of the list. However, this might not be the order in which you want them to appear. You can add them in the order you want them to appear, or you can simply move them around after they are in the list.

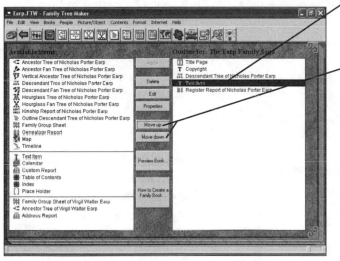

1. In the Outline for list, **click** on the **tree or report** you want to move. The item will be highlighted.

2. Click on the **Move up or Move down button** to move the highlighted item.

> ### NOTE
>
> Although Family Tree Maker doesn't disable the buttons, you cannot move the Title Page. Family Tree Maker will tell you that the Title Page must be the first item in the book.

Working with Item Properties

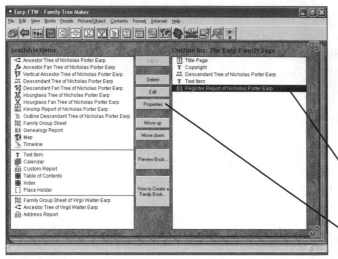

As you were putting your reports and trees into the order in which they now appear, you were probably visualizing the divisions of your book. If you look at any of the published family histories in your local genealogy library, you will see that they are broken into chapters to make the book easier to use.

1. Click on the **report or tree** with which you want to work. The report or tree will be highlighted.

2. Click on the **Properties button**. The Item Properties dialog box will open.

3. Select the **This item begins a Chapter check box** if you want the item to be the first item in a new chapter. A check mark will appear in the check box.

4. Select the **Start this item on odd numbered page check box** if you want to control on what page this item will begin. A check mark will appear in the check box.

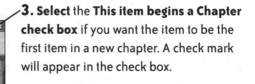

TIP

You can use the Header/Footer options to determine which of your reports and trees will include the header or footer information. The header is usually the title of the book. The footer is usually the page number.

5. Click on **OK**. Your changes will be saved and the Item Properties dialog box will close.

Finalizing the Book

Family Tree Maker offers a few features to help to define your book and make it easier to read. After all, you want those who read the book to find it easy to use.

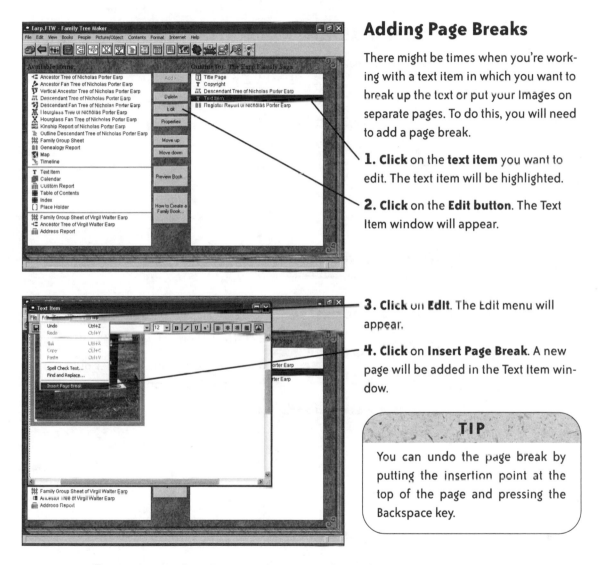

Adding Page Breaks

There might be times when you're working with a text item in which you want to break up the text or put your Images on separate pages. To do this, you will need to add a page break.

1. Click on the **text item** you want to edit. The text item will be highlighted.

2. Click on the **Edit button**. The Text Item window will appear.

3. Click on **Edit**. The Edit menu will appear.

4. Click on **Insert Page Break**. A new page will be added in the Text Item window.

TIP

You can undo the page break by putting the insertion point at the top of the page and pressing the Backspace key.

---

5. Click on the **Close button**. Family Tree Maker will prompt you to save the changes and the Text Item window will close.

Creating a Customized Index

Family Tree Maker allows you to include an index in your family history book. Genealogists for years to come will be pleased to find that your book has an index. While Family Tree Maker does the hard work of organizing the page numbers, you control the look and feel of the index.

1. Click on **Index** in the Available items list. The option will be highlighted.

2. Click on **Add**. The index will be added to the end of the Outline for list.

3. In the Outline for list, **click** on **Index**. The option will be highlighted.

4. Click on **Edit**. The Index of Individuals Report will appear.

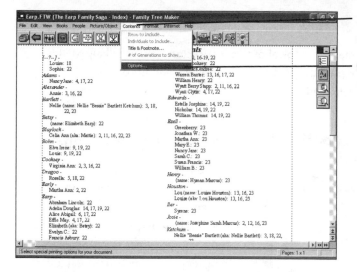

5. Click on **Contents**. The Contents menu will appear.

6. Click on **Options**. The Options for Book Index dialog box will open.

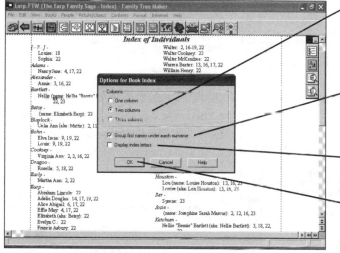

7. Click on the **Columns radio button** to select the number of columns to include in the index. The option will be selected.

8. Click on the **Group first names under each surname check box**. A check mark will appear.

9. Click on the **Display index letters check box**. A check mark will appear.

10. Click on **OK**. Family Tree Maker will make the requested changes to the report.

TIP

You might want to view the index with all possible combinations of these choices to examine the effect each combination has on the ease of reading the index.

Sharing Your Book

Once you have spent time creating a book about your ancestors, you will likely want to share it. You may just want to print the book for a few family members or you may want to share it on CD-ROM for many to read.

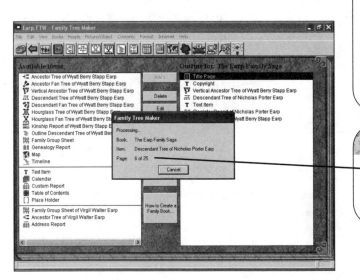

Previewing Your Book

Before going through the exercise of printing your book, you may want to take advantage of the option in Family Tree Maker that lets you preview your book. This is a great way to see if everything looks the way you want it to before you actually commit it to print.

1. Click on **Preview Book...** Family Tree Maker will begin to compile your book and then will launch Adobe Acrobat Reader.

TIP

In order to take advantage of the Preview Book option, you will need to have Adobe's Acrobat Reader, a free software program from Adobe (http://www.adobe.com/), installed on your computer.

NOTE

You can get an idea of how big your book will be as Family Tree Maker is compiling it.

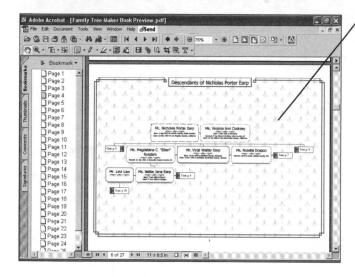

2. View the **compiled book** to see if any changes need to be made.

Printing Your Book

Once you have previewed your book and are happy with the way it looks, you are then ready to send it to the printer. Once you have a printed copy you can take it to a photocopy shop to get as many copies as you need, rather than putting all that wear and tear on your printer.

1. Click on **File**. The File menu will appear.

2. Click on **Print Book**. The Print Book dialog box will open.

3. Click on **Print color**. The trees and images in color will print in color, provided you have a color printer.

4. Click on **Mirror margins**. The margins will be adjusted for binding in a book.

5. Determine the **number of copies**.

6. Click on **OK**. Family Tree Maker will begin to compile the book for printing.

Exporting Your Book to PDF

You may find that there are many people who are interested in your book. One of the best distribution options available is to save the book as a PDF (Portable Document Format) and then put it on a CD-ROM to share. Anyone wanting to view your book this way will need to have the Adobe Acrobat Reader.

1. Click on **File**. The File menu will appear.

2. Move the **mouse pointer** to **Export Book**. The Export Book submenu will appear.

3. Click on **To Acrobat (PDF)**. The Export Books dialog box will open.

4. Type the **name** of the file in the File name field.

5. Click on the **Save button**. The book will be saved.

TIP

Don't forget to pay attention to where Family Tree Maker is saving the file so you can find it later.

19

Creating Your Personal Family Tree Maker Home Page

While publishing a family history is still traditionally done by putting it on paper, the Internet provides a marvelous new way for people to publish their family histories. When publishing to paper, people tend to hold off publishing in an effort to get everything perfect. The Internet saves people from this need to delay, as they can always upload a revised version of their pages. In this chapter, you'll learn how to:

- Create your first home page

- Register your home page

- Add reports to your home page

- Add trees to your home page

- Remove items from your home page

Creating Your First Home Page

Computers can intimidate genealogists, and many genealogists consider the Internet to be the biggest computer of them all. Fortunately Family Tree Maker has a wizard that makes creating your first family history webpage on Genealogy.com an easy and enjoyable experience. It is not necessary to understand anything about the Internet or computers. The wizard walks you through each step in the creation of your home page.

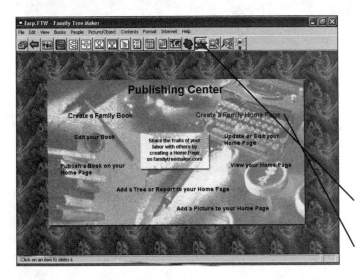

Working with the Wizard

Family Tree Maker, like many other software programs, is adding wizards that help you perform certain tasks. The Family Home Page wizard walks you through putting together a basic home page that will be displayed at Genealogy.com.

1. Click on the **Publishing Center button**. The Publishing Center will appear.

2. Click on **Create a Family Home Page**. The Family Home Page wizard will appear.

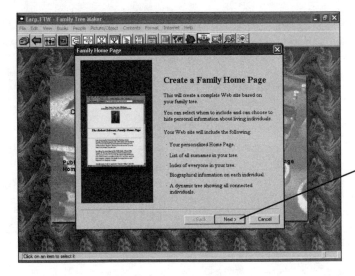

NOTE

The Family Home Page wizard helps you learn how to create a family history home page on the Family Tree Maker website.

3. Click on the **Next button**. The wizard will begin to ask you questions.

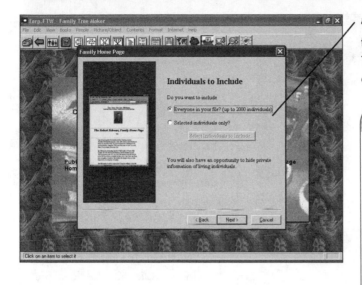

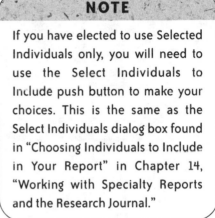

4. Select between **Everyone in your file** and **Selected Individuals only?** The radio button will move to your desired selection.

> ### NOTE
>
> If you have elected to use Selected Individuals only, you will need to use the Select Individuals to Include push button to make your choices. This is the same as the Select Individuals dialog box found in "Choosing Individuals to Include in Your Report" in Chapter 14, "Working with Specialty Reports and the Research Journal."

5. Click on **Next**. The wizard will ask the next question. Continue to answer the questions of the wizard.

> ### TIP
>
> One of the wizard questions asks about hiding the information on living individuals. It is a good idea to select the Hide Info on Living Individuals option. Many people are nervous about identity theft in today's high tech world. Omitting personal information about living individuals from your website also protects against any invasion of their privacy.

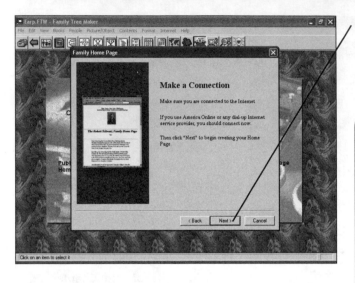

6. Make sure you are **connected to the Internet** and then **click** on **Next**. The Uploading Homepage status bar will appear.

> ### TIP
>
> The Status bar lets you know how much of your page has already been uploaded. When it has finished uploading you will get a message box telling you of the success of the upload and that the information will be on the Internet within 15 minutes. Click OK to close the message box.

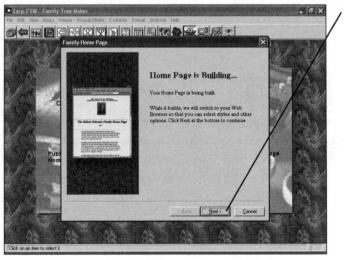

7. Click on **Next**. Family Tree Maker will launch your Web browser and the Create Your Own webpage will open.

Selecting a Theme for Your Home Page

The wizard has put together a general page for you to upload. Once the initial information has been collected and uploaded by Family Tree Maker, you will find that the Create Your Own Home Page will get some specifics about you and how you want the website to look.

1. Type in the **title** that you want to appear on your webpage and then **press** the **Tab key**. The cursor will move to the first field of the Contact Information section.

2a. Click on the **Do not include my name on my home page box**. The check mark will appear and your name will not be included on the webpage.

OR

2b. Leave the **Do not include my name on my home page box** empty and **press** the **Tab** key to move to the name section of the Contact information.

3. Type in **your name** in the three name fields, **pressing** the **Tab** key to move from one field to the next.

4. Continue to **supply** information in the Contact Information section.

TIP

Because this is being posted to the Internet, it is often a good idea to elect not to include your address or phone number on the site. Be sure though to include your e-mail address so that those who come upon your information can get in contact with you. You never know when a cousin will have information to share.

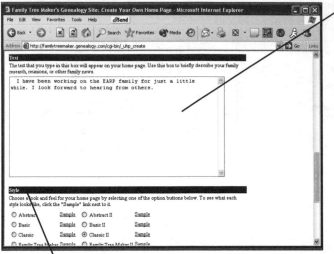

5. Describe your website in the Text box and then **press** the **Tab** key. The cursor will move to the Style section.

> **NOTE**
>
> The Text section is where you will want to include information about your research and your purpose for doing the research. It is the introduction that visitors to your site will read, so it is their first impression of you and what you are doing with your research.

6. Choose a **Style** for your webpage. The radio button will move to that style.

> **TIP**
>
> If you click on the Sample link your browser will show you an example of that style theme. Simply use the Back button in your browser software to return to the Create Your Own Home Page page and finish your style selection.

7. Click on the **Create Home Page Now button**. The page will be created and shown in your browser and the Personal Mail List window will open.

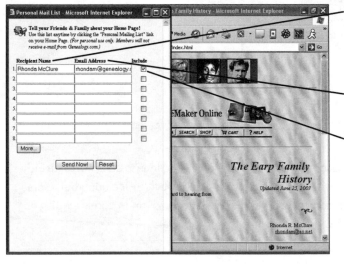

8. Type in the **Recipient's name** in the Recipient Name field and **press** the **Tab** key. The cursor will move to the E-mail Address field.

9. Type in the **E-mail address** for the recipient in the E-mail Address field.

10. Click on the **Include check box**. The individual will be included in the e-mail message sent alerting them about your new webpage.

TIP

The Personal Mail List is a great way to share with cousins when your combined work is ready for display. While the initial screen displays the places for e-mail addresses of eight of your cousins, you are not limited to just those fields. Clicking on the More button offers additional space to add more cousins' names and e-mail addresses.

---

11. Click on the **Send Now button**. A message box will appear telling you that the message has been sent.

Working with Your Home Page

After the wizard has helped you upload that first webpage, you can enhance it by adding additional reports, an InterneTree, or even a book. The beauty of your home page is that you can change what is available whenever you wish. Most of the reports that you can print to paper can be posted to your Family Tree Maker site as well.

Adding Reports

Adding reports to your family home page will make them viewable to anyone who visits your webpage. These pages will be added to the indexing and searching functions found on Family Tree Maker's website and to the Genealogy.com search page. There are many reports and trees that you can publish to your family home page, including

- Outline Descendant Trees

- Custom Reports

- Genealogy Reports (Register, NGSQ, or Ahnentafel)

- Family Tree Maker Book

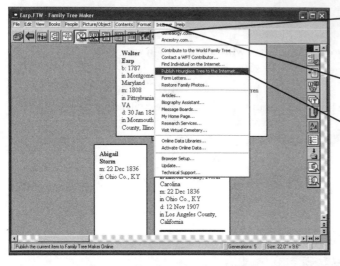

1. Click on the **report button** for the tree or report you want to add to your home page. The report will appear.

2. Click on **Internet**. The Internet menu will appear.

3. Click on **Publish Report to the Internet**. The Add a Tree to Your Home Page wizard will open.

TIP

Some trees, such as the Standard Ancestor Tree, will prompt Family Tree Maker to upload an InterneTree and a PDF version of the ancestor tree chart if you want. The PDF version looks like the printed tree, whereas the InterneTree is an interactive pedigree that visitors can navigate through when looking at your research online.

---

4. Answer the **question** asked. The wizard will record the answer.

5. Click on **Next**. The wizard will ask the next question.

6. Continue to answer the wizard's **questions**. When it has asked all the questions, the last page of the wizard will have a Finish button, that once clicked will upload the report to your Web space at Genealogy.com.

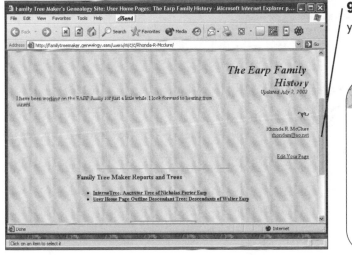

7. Click on the **Publishing Center button**. The Publishing Center will appear.

8. Click on **View your Home Page**. Your browser will appear.

9. Use the **scroll bar** to scan through your webpage.

NOTE

You will see that, in addition to working in the Family Tree Maker program, you can also upload other items to your home page, including pictures and Web links. Click on the Add to or Edit This Section link to customize your home page.

Adding an InterneTree

An InterneTree is a box-style tree. However, unlike the normal box-style reports, this one is interactive. Visitors to your home page can use an index and move through the generations. For each person in the tree, they will see the name, birth date, and death date for the individual.

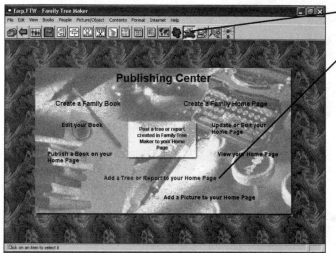

1. Click on the **Publishing Center button**. The Publishing Center will appear.

2. Click on **Add a Tree or Report to Your Home Page**. The Add a Tree or Report to Your Home Page dialog box will open.

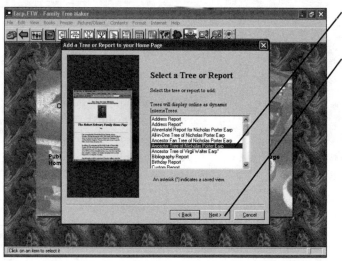

3. Select an appropriate **tree report**. The report will be selected.

4. Click on the **Next button**. The Select a Tree options will appear.

NOTE

If you wish to share all of your database in the InterneTree, the best tree report to select would be the All-in-One tree.

NOTE

You can have only one InterneTree on your site at a time. If you would like other tree reports to be available as well, you will need to select the Graphical Tree option when uploading them.

5a. **Select** the **InterneTree**. The radio button will move to the InterneTree.

OR

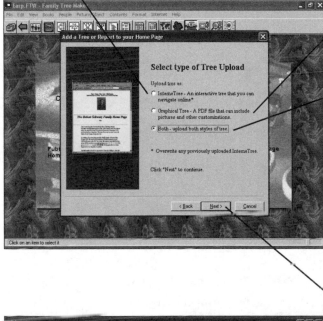

5b. **Select** the **Graphical Tree**. The radio button will move to the Graphical Tree.

OR

5c. **Select** the **Both** option. The radio button will move to the Both option.

TIP

At the present time an InterneTree can have up to 2,000 individuals in it. This is important to remember if you have chosen to upload a report that includes all the individuals in your database.

6. Click on **Next**. The wizard will ask a few more questions before finishing. The tree will then be published to the Internet.

NOTE

You might need to click on the Refresh button in your browser to see the InterneTree in the list of reports on your home page.

Adding a Book

Just as you can print a family history book and send it to your family and fellow researchers, you can also include it on your home page. This offers you the chance to publish your book while it's still a work in progress. As you find new information or correct inaccurate conclusions, you can simply upload a new version of the book to your home page.

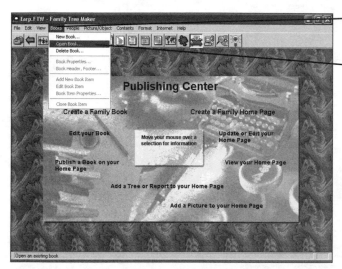

1. Click on **Books**. The Books menu will appear.

2. Click on **Open Book**. The Open Book dialog box will open.

3. Select the **book** you want from the Available books list. The book will be highlighted.

4. Click on **OK**. The Book window will appear.

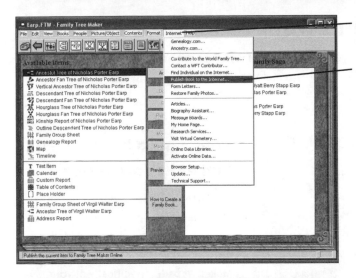

5. Click on **Internet**. The Internet menu will appear.

6. Click on **Publish Book to the Internet**. Family Tree Maker will upload the book, as it has already been designed, to your home page.

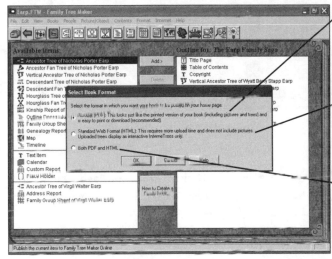

7a. Select the **Acrobat** radio button. Family Tree Maker will publish a PDF version of the book to your home page.

OR

7b. Select the **Standard Web Format** radio button. Family Tree Maker will publish an HTML (Web) version of the book to your home page.

OR

7c. Select the **Both PDF and HTML** radio button. Family Tree Maker will publish both the PDF and the HTML (Web) versions of the book to your home page.

NOTE

During this process you may be prompted to add a Table of Contents if your book did not have one yet. You will also be asked if you want to contribute to the World Family Tree. Click Yes if you do or No if you do not. World Family Tree is a compilation of GED-COM submissions by researchers interested in sharing their information on the World Family Tree CD-ROMs.

Removing Items from Your Home Page

Don't think that just because your Family Tree Maker program has uploaded these pages, you have no control over whether they remain on the home page. You determine what stays online.

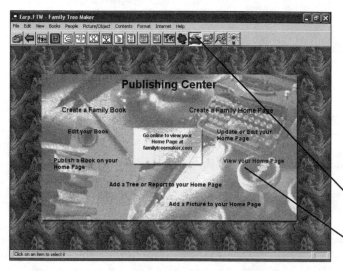

Removing a Family Tree Maker Report or Book

Removing a report or book that you have placed on your home page is not done through the Family Tree Maker program. This is done at the Family Tree Maker website, specifically at your home page.

1. Click on the **Publishing Center button**. The Publishing Center will open.

2. Click on **View your Home Page**. Your browser will open and you will be taken to your home page.

3. Click on **Edit Your Page**. The Author Options page will open in your browser.

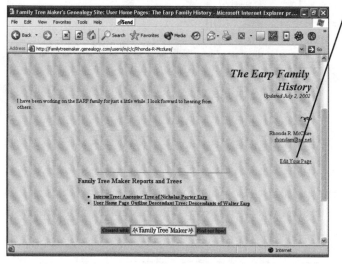

4. Scroll to the **Remove Information section** at the bottom of the edit page and **click** on the **link** for the information you want to remove. The Removing page will appear.

5. Click on the **check box** next to the item you wish to remove. A check mark will appear.

6. Click on the **Remove Selected Items button**. The item(s) will be removed.

Deleting Your Home Page

You are not limited to removing specific items from your home page. You can also delete the entire home page—if necessary. You can always re-create it at a later date.

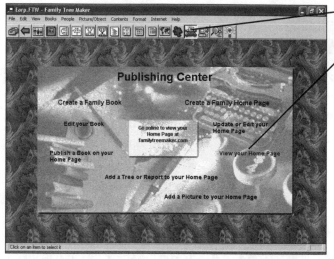

1. Click on the **Publishing Center button**. The Publishing Center will appear.

2. Click on **View Your Home Page**. Your browser will open and take you to your home page.

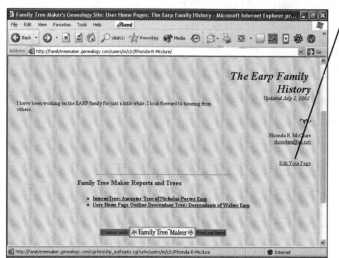

3. Click on **Edit Your Page**. The Author Options webpage will appear.

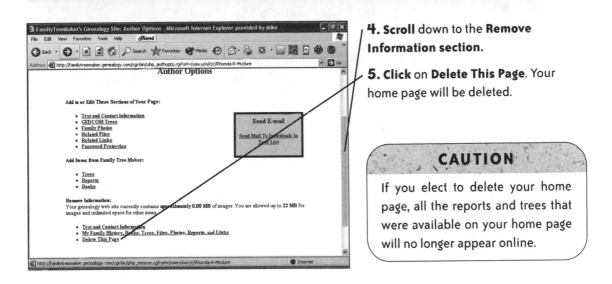

4. Scroll down to the **Remove Information section.**

5. Click on **Delete This Page**. Your home page will be deleted.

CAUTION

If you elect to delete your home page, all the reports and trees that were available on your home page will no longer appear online.

PART
VI

Advanced Family Tree Maker Methods

Chapter 20
Working with Dates and
Facts 323

Chapter 21
Working with GEDCOM Files and Other Family Files ...337

Chapter 22
Working with Family Tree Maker Preferences 361

Chapter 23
Enhancing Your Family History Book 375

20

Working with Dates and Facts

Working with the Marriage field in the Family Page might overshadow some of the other features you have used in the More About Marriage Facts window. Custom facts offer you an unlimited number of life events, though as your experience with the program grows, you might want to do away with some of the facts you have created. In this chapter, you'll learn how to:

- Work with the marriage fact

- Coordinate the Marriage Fact and More About Marriage Facts options

- Remove a previously created custom fact name

- Work with the date calculator to estimate dates

Working with the Marriage Fact

It is almost second nature, as a genealogist, to want to enter a date of marriage for the parents of a family. Understanding how Family Tree Maker works with the information submitted here will prevent frustration when you are generating reports.

It is extremely tempting to fill in an approximate date in the Marriage date field on the Family Page. The Marriage date field, however, should be reserved for those times when you have an actual marriage date, for instance when you have in your possession (or when you have seen) a marriage license or certificate.

Understanding Beginning Status

The Beginning status field can be ignored if you wish. If you are not entering information into the Marriage date field, the beginning status field might prove useful in helping you to remember what you know about that couple's relationship.

1. Click on the **Beginning status down arrow**. The Beginning status drop-down list will appear.

> **TIP**
>
> If you hold the mouse pointer over the Beginning status field, a pop-up Help message will appear, explaining the purpose of this option in Family Tree Maker.

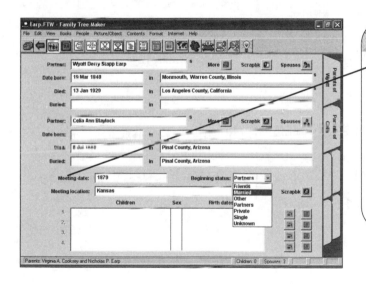

2. Click on the **appropriate status**. The status will be selected.

Notice how the wording for the Marriage date and place have changed based on the new beginning status option. In some reports, this will change the wording of the reports from "married" to "met." On the Family Page, you will see that the word "marriage" has now been changed to "meeting."

Getting Family Page and More About Marriage Facts to Work Together

You will want to pay close attention to the options in the Beginning status menu. When selecting from the More About Marriage Facts menu, you will need to select a preferred marriage fact.

1. Click on the **Family Page button**. The Family Page will appear.

2. Click on the **Beginning status down arrow**. The Beginning status drop-down menu will appear.

3. Select the **Married** status from the list. The option will be selected.

NOTE

Be sure that the Marriage date and Marriage location fields are empty on the Family Page.

4. Type the **marriage date and place**. Make note of the date and place.

5. Click on the **More button**. The More About Marriage window will appear.

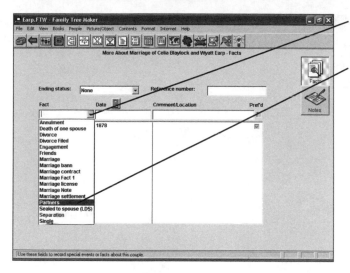

6. Click on the **Fact down arrow**. The Fact drop-down menu will appear.

7. Click on **Partners**. The Partners fact will be selected.

8. Press the **Tab key**. The cursor will move to the Date field.

9. Type the **date** and **press** the **Tab key.** The cursor will move to Comment/Location field.

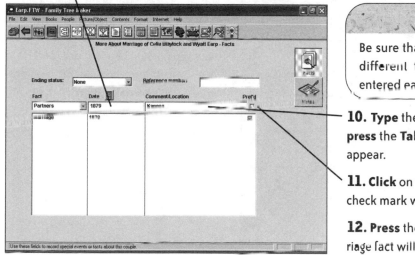

TIP

Be sure that the date in question is different than the marriage date entered earlier.

10. Type the **place or comment** and **press** the **Tab key**. The cursor will disappear.

11. Click on the **Pref'd check box**. A check mark will appear.

12. Press the **Tab key**. The new marriage fact will be placed in the event list.

13. Click on the **Family Page button**.

The Family Page will open. Notice that the Family Page has changed. The Marriage date and location fields have been renamed to Meeting date and Meeting location. The date information reflects the new date entered. Also, notice that the Beginning status reflects the Partners selection.

Removing a Custom Fact Name

One of the questions Family Tree Maker users often ask pertains to custom facts that they create and then want to delete.

Verifying No One Is Using the Fact

Before you can do anything with the custom fact name in your Fact list, you must first verify that no one in the database is still linked to the fact.

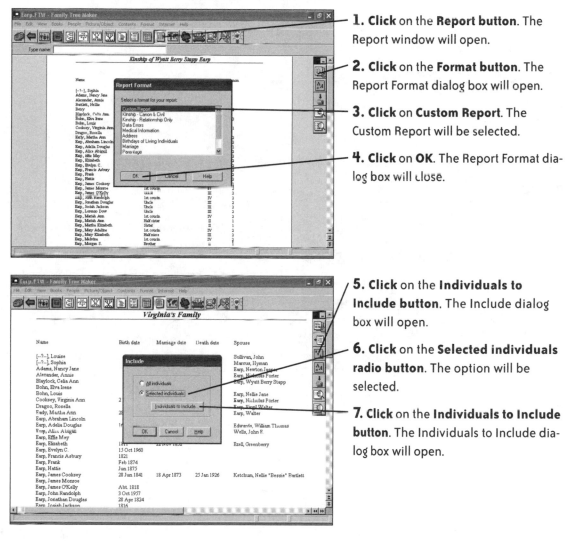

1. Click on the **Report button**. The Report window will open.

2. Click on the **Format button**. The Report Format dialog box will open.

3. Click on **Custom Report**. The Custom Report will be selected.

4. Click on **OK**. The Report Format dialog box will close.

5. Click on the **Individuals to Include button**. The Include dialog box will open.

6. Click on the **Selected individuals radio button**. The option will be selected.

7. Click on the **Individuals to Include button**. The Individuals to Include dialog box will open.

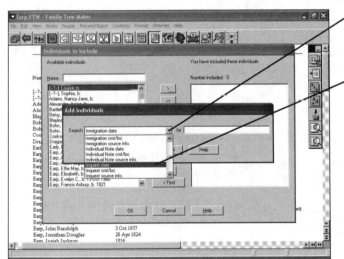

TIP

If there are individuals in the You have included these individuals list, click on the << button to remove them from the list.

8. Click on the **Find> button**. The Add Individuals dialog box will open.

9. Click on the **Search down arrow**. The Search drop-down menu will appear.

10. Select the **fact** you wish to remove. The fact will be selected.

11. Press the **Tab key**. The cursor will move to the for field.

12. Type !=.

NOTE

By entering the characters != you are telling Family Tree Maker to show you anyone with anything in that field. This is the best way to find anyone still associated with the fact.

13. Click on **OK**. The Add Individuals dialog box will close.

14. Click on **OK**. The Individuals to Include dialog box will close.

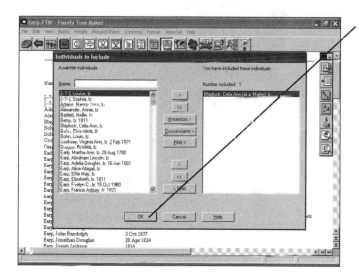

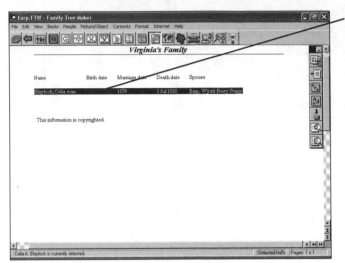

15. Double-click on **one of the names** that appears in the report. The Individual Facts Card will open.

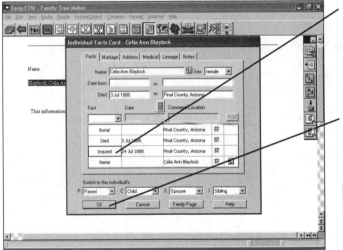

16. Click on the **fact**. The fact will be highlighted.

17. Press the **Delete key.** The fact will be removed from the list of facts for that individual.

18. Click on **OK.** The Individual Facts Card will close.

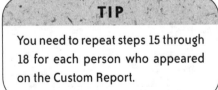

TIP

You need to repeat steps 15 through 18 for each person who appeared on the Custom Report.

Think Rename, Not Delete

Once you no longer have anyone using the fact, you can get rid of it. You won't actually be deleting the fact; instead, you'll be renaming it. Before beginning this section, be sure to be in the More About Facts window for anyone in your database.

1. Click on the **Fact down arrow**. The Fact drop-down menu will appear.

2. Select the **fact to be removed** and **press** the **Tab key**. The fact will be selected and the cursor will move to the Date field.

3. Type a **date** and **press** the **Tab key** twice. The fact will be added to the More About Facts window.

NOTE

In order for Family Tree Maker to recognize the fact, you must enter either a date or a place. Hitting the Tab key three times will not allow you to add an empty fact to the list. The fact must be added to the list before you can change its name.

4. Highlight the **name** of the fact to be deleted. That fact name will be selected.

5. Type the **name** of one of the unused facts in the Fact list. The name of the fact will change.

TIP

The Family Tree Maker KnowledgeBase at Genealogy.com suggests changing a fact to be deleted to the Caste event, as this is not often used in your general research.

6. Press the **Tab key**. The Change Fact Name message box will appear.

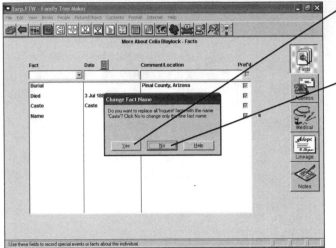

7a. Click on **Yes**. The fact name will be changed.

OR

7b. Click on **No**. The fact name will not be changed.

8. Click on the **newly named fact**. The fact will be highlighted.

9. Press the **Delete key**. The fact name will be deleted.

10. Press the **Tab key**. The fact will be removed from the individual's list of facts.

Calculating Dates or Ages

There are times when you discover the age of an individual included in records. Through this information you can calculate the date of birth of the person. At other times you may not know the date of death but you have his age at death. When combined with the date of birth you can calculate the date of death.

TIP

You have access to the date calculator any time you are in a date field in the Family Page. You will see a similar date calculator icon in the More About Facts page as well as in the Individual Facts Card. You can also access the date calculator by clicking on the People menu and selecting the Date Calculator.

1. Click in the **date field** you want to calculate. The date calculator icon will appear.

2. Click on the **date calculator**. The Date Calculator dialog box will appear.

3. Type in the **date** of the **known event**.

4. Press the **Tab key** twice. The cursor will move to the Age at time of event field.

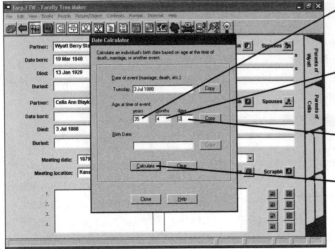

5. Type in the **number of years** in the years field and press Tab. The cursor will move to the months field.

6. Type in the **number of months** in the months field and press Tab. The cursor will move to the days field.

7. Type in the **number of days** in the days field.

8. Click on the **Calculate button**. Family Tree Maker will calculate the date of birth.

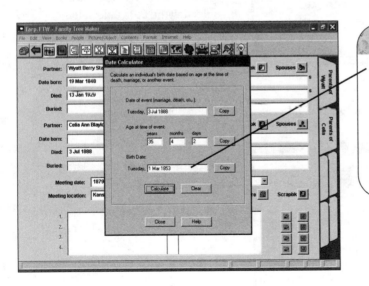

NOTE

If you want to calculate the date of death, you would put in the Birth date and the age at time of event field and leave the Date of event field empty. Clicking on the Calculate would then supply you with the date of death.

21

Working with GEDCOM Files and Other Family Files

At some point in your research you may get a database from another researcher or want to share yours with another. Such sharing is usually done through GEDCOM files. There will also be times when you will want to keep some of your research in a separate Family File, or compare two files. In this chapter, you'll learn how to:

- Export a complete Family File using GEDCOM

- Export a partial Family File using GED-COM

- Import a GEDCOM file to an existing Family File

- Open two Family Files to compare

- Copy and paste from one Family File to another

Creating a GEDCOM File

When it comes time to share with other researchers, the easiest way to share your information is through a GEDCOM file. This allows researchers to import your work regardless of whether or not they are using Family Tree Maker.

Sharing Your Complete Family File

When sharing with others in your immediate family, you will probably want to share your entire database.

1. Click on the **Family Page button**. The Family Page will appear.

2. Click on **File**. The File menu will appear.

3. Click on **Copy/Export Family File**. The New Family File dialog box will open.

NOTE

While Family Tree Maker allows you to add digitized images, sounds, and objects, these links are not supported by GEDCOM. If you share a GEDCOM file, the scrapbook images will not be included in the GEDCOM file.

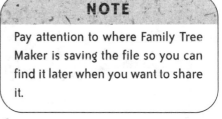

4. Click on the **Save as type down arrow**. The Save as type menu will appear.

5. Click on **GEDCOM (*.GED)**. The GED-COM option will be selected.

TIP

Family Tree Maker automatically names the GEDCOM file with the same name you gave the Family File originally. You can double-click on this name to highlight it and type a new name if you want.

NOTE

Pay attention to where Family Tree Maker is saving the file so you can find it later when you want to share it.

6. Click on the **Save button**. The Export to GEDCOM dialog box will open.

NOTE

Generally the default settings will work when sharing a GEDCOM file. However, if you are a Latter-Day Saint creating a file for TempleReady, you will want to use the Destination drop-down menu to select TempleReady.

7. Click on **OK**. The Export to GEDCOM dialog box will close and the file will be saved.

Sharing Part of a Family File

Usually when you are sharing with individuals you have met through a genealogical society or on the Internet, you will only want to send them the line that you share in common.

TIP

To determine the individual to select, first you need to determine the line you want to share. Find the child of that line in the Index of Individuals.

1. Press the **F2 key**. The Index of Individuals dialog box will open.

2. Click on the **appropriate individual**. He or she will be selected.

3. Click on **OK**. The Index of Individuals dialog box will close.

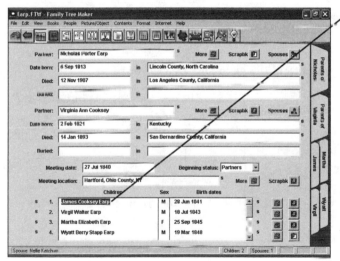

4. Click on the **Parents of tab** for the spouse of the selected individual. The Family Page will display the new family.

5. Click on the **spouse as a child**. The child will be highlighted.

6. Click on **People**. The People menu will appear.

7. Move the **mouse pointer** to Fix Relationship Mistakes. The Fix Relationship Mistakes menu will appear.

8. Click on **Detach Child**. The child will be detached from his or her parents.

NOTE

For a refresher on how to detach a child, see Chapter 12, "Fixing Relationships and Duplicates." In this case, you are temporarily detaching the child. You do not want to detach the siblings.

9. Use the **Index of Individuals** to relocate the individual selected in step 2.

10. Click on the **All-in-One Tree button**. The All-in-One Tree will open.

11. Click on the **Options button**. The Options for All-in-One Tree dialog box will open.

TIP

While this example is using the All-in-One Tree to isolate the desired individuals, you can also create a list of individuals using the Custom Report. For detailed information on searching for individuals to include in the Custom Report, see Chapter 14, "Working with Specialty Reports and the Research Journal."

12. Click on the **Show unconnected step-family trees check box**. The option will be selected.

13. Click on **OK**. The Options for All-in-One Tree dialog box will close.

14. Click on **File**. The File menu will appear.

15. Click on **Copy/Export Individuals in Tree**. The Copy/Export Individuals in All-in-One Tree dialog box will open.

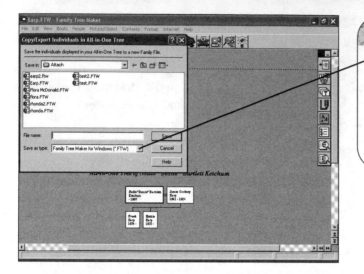

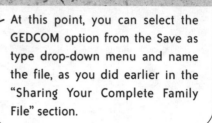

NOTE

At this point, you can select the GEDCOM option from the Save as type drop-down menu and name the file, as you did earlier in the "Sharing Your Complete Family File" section.

Importing a GEDCOM File into an Existing Family File

Just as you will share GEDCOM files, you will also receive them. You can import a GEDCOM file directly into your Family File. However, this must be done from the Family Page.

TIP

Before beginning this process, it is a good idea to save your Family File as a backup, either by copying it elsewhere on your hard drive or by selecting Backup Family File from the File menu, which is discussed later in this chapter under "Saving a Backup of Your Family File."

1. Click on **File**. The File menu will appear.

2. Click on **Append/Merge Family File**. The Append Family File dialog box will open.

NOTE

Before you add someone's GEDCOM file to your Family File, it is a good idea to first create a new Family File of the data. This allows you to evaluate the data before it gets mixed in your own Family File. Once you have determined its accuracy, you can then follow the steps in this section to add it to your personal Family File. To see how to create a new Family File with a GEDCOM file, see the "Opening a GEDCOM File as a New Family File" section later in this chapter.

3. Click on the **Files of type down arrow**. The Files of Type menu will appear.

4. Click on **GEDCOM (*.GED)**. The GEDCOM file type will be selected.

TIP

These same steps can be used to append someone else's Family File or another one you have created. Instead of selecting GEDCOM (*.GED) from the Files of type menu, you would select Family Tree Maker for Windows (*.FTW).

5. Click on the **appropriate GEDCOM file**. The file will be selected.

6. Click on **OK**. The warning message will close and the Import from GEDCOM dialog box will open.

7. Click on the **Facts to import button**. The Facts to Import dialog box will open.

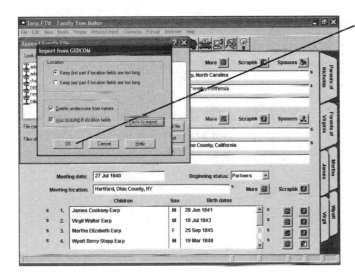

NOTE

It is a good idea to look and see where Family Tree Maker wants to put some of the facts that will be imported. This is even more important when the GEDCOM file you are importing is coming from someone who is not using Family Tree Maker.

8. Click on **OK**. The Facts to Import dialog box will close.

9. Click on **OK**. The Import from GEDCOM dialog box will close, the GEDCOM file will be appended to the Family File, and a message box will open.

10. Click on **OK**. The message box will close and the Individuals to Include dialog box will open.

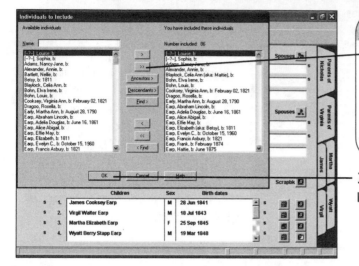

This dialog box is the same as the one you were introduced to in Chapter 10, "Searching Your Family Tree File." Usually you will select everyone in the GEDCOM file using the [>>] button.

11. Click on **OK**. The Append File dialog box will open.

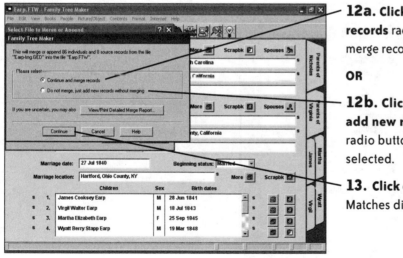

12a. Click on the **Continue and merge records** radio button. The Continue and merge records option will be selected.

OR

12b. Click on the **Do not merge, just add new records without merging** radio button. This option will be selected.

13. Click on **Continue**. The Likely Matches dialog box will open.

If you need a refresher on how to check the Family File for duplicates, see Chapter 12, "Fixing Relationships and Duplicates."

Opening a GEDCOM File as a New Family File

In addition to appending a GEDCOM file to an existing Family File, you can also create a new Family File using a GEDCOM file as the source of the data.

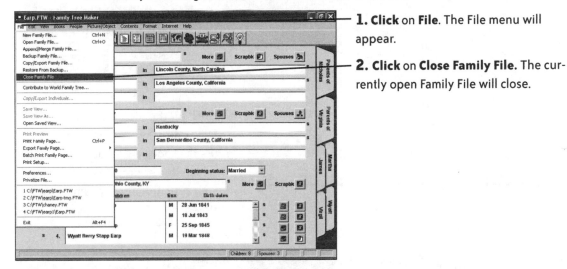

1. Click on **File**. The File menu will appear.

2. Click on **Close Family File**. The currently open Family File will close.

3. Click on **File**. The File menu will appear.

4. Click on **Open Family File**. The Open Family File dialog box will open.

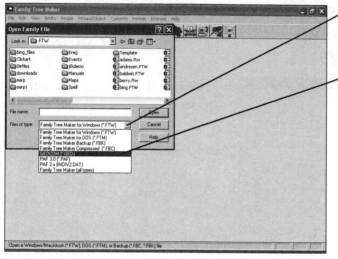

5. Click on the **Files of type down arrow**. The Files of type menu will appear.

6. Click on **GEDCOM (*.GED)**. The GED-COM file type will be selected.

> ### NOTE
>
> If you have not saved your Family Files in the default Family Tree Maker directory, you might need to use the Look in drop-down menu to select the appropriate folder on your system where the Family File is stored.

7. Click on the **appropriate GEDCOM file**. The file will be selected.

8. Click on the **Open button**. The New Family File dialog box will open.

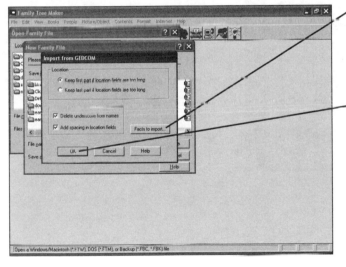

9. Type the **name** of the new Family File.

10. Click on the **Save button**. The Import from GEDCOM dialog box will open.

11a. Click on the **Facts to import button**. The Facts to Import dialog box will open.

OR

11b. Click on **OK**. A message box will appear, telling you the import is complete.

12. If you followed Step 11b, **click** on **OK** to close the message box and go into the new Family File.

Opening Two Family Files

As your research progresses, it is conceivable that you might have more than one Family File. You might decide to create a Family File for a single-surname study or to keep a record of all those individuals to whom you haven't been able to figure out a connection. Once those Family Files are created, there may come a time when you wish to have two files open simultaneously for comparison or importing of individuals from one Family File to the other.

Using the Open Family File Option

With a Family File already open, you can use the Open Family File option to open another Family File to compare or double check information in the other file.

1. Click on **File**. The File menu will appear.

2. Click on **Open Family File**. The Open Family File dialog box will open.

> **TIP**
>
> You can also open the Open Family File dialog box by pressing Ctrl+O.

3. Click on the **Family File** you want to open. The file will be selected.

4. Click on the **Open button**. The Family File will open.

Using File History

Family Tree Maker will remember the last four Family Files you worked with, including the presently open Family File. You can access this history list to open a previous Family File.

1. Click on **File**. The File menu will appear.

2. Click on the **desired Family File**. That Family File will open in another Family Tree Maker window.

Copying and Pasting Between Family Files

When you have two Family Files open, you can work between the two of them, copying individuals or text from one to the other. Make sure that you have opened two Family Files using one of the methods just discussed.

1. Click on the **individual** you want to copy. The individual will be selected.

2. Click on **Edit**. The Edit menu will appear.

3. Move your **mouse pointer** over **Copy**. The Copy submenu will appear.

4. Click on **Copy Selected Individual**. The person's information is placed on the clipboard.

NOTE

Family Tree Maker offers many different options for copying information. In addition to limiting the copy to just the selected individual, you can also copy the information for everyone on the family page, the highlighted individual and all his ancestors, or the highlighted individual and all her descendants.

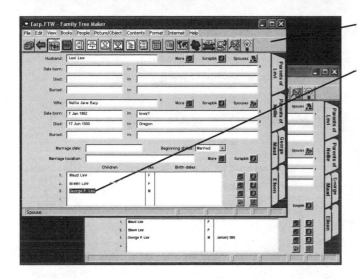

5. Click on the **other** Family File. The Family File becomes the active file.

6. Click on the **individual** or **field** where you want to put the information. This will be selected.

7. Click on **Edit**. The Edit menu will appear.

8. Click on **Paste Individuals**. Family Tree Maker will verify that you wish to paste the information or that the correct individual has been selected in the new Family File and then the Merge Individuals window will open.

Saving a Backup of Your Family File

It is a good idea to save a backup of your family file from time to time. If you have added a lot of new information or new individuals, that is a perfect time to create a backup so that all your hard work is not lost, should something go wrong.

1. Click on **File**. The File menu will appear.

2. Click on **Backup Family File**. The Backup Family File dialog box will open.

> ## NOTE
>
> You will need to save the backup file somewhere. It is easiest to save to your hard drive. You should, however, also copy that backup file to another medium, e.g., a floppy disk, a CD-ROM disc, or the Internet, so that you have it in more than one place should something happen.

3a. Click on **Floppy Drive**. The radio button will move to Floppy Drive.

OR

3b. Click on **Writable CD Drive**

OR

3c. Click on **Working Directory**. The radio button will move to Working Directory.

OR

3d. Click on **Custom Directory**. The radio button will move to Custom Directory.

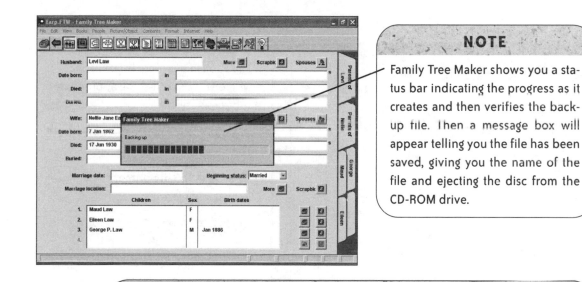

NOTE

If you select the Custom Directory, you can use the Change push button to select the directory you would like to use or change the name of the file.

4. If you have selected the Writable CD, be sure that you have put a writable disc in the CD-R or CD-RW drive, then **click** on **OK**. Family Tree Maker will begin to back up the family file to the CD.

NOTE

Family Tree Maker shows you a status bar indicating the progress as it creates and then verifies the backup file. Then a message box will appear telling you the file has been saved, giving you the name of the file and ejecting the disc from the CD-ROM drive.

TIP

The first time you select the writable CD option, Family Tree Maker may need to install additional files to your computer to allow it to write to the disc.

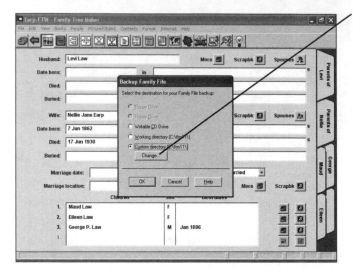

5. If you have selected the Custom Directory, **click** on **Change** to select the appropriate sub-directory or change the name of the file. The Change filename or directory window will open.

6. Click on the **Look in down arrow**. The Look in directory list will appear where you can select the appropriate sub-directory.

7. Double click in the **File name field**. The file name will be selected.

8. Type in the **file name**. The name of the backup file will change.

> **TIP**
>
> You will not want to change the .FBC extension of the file name. This is a necessary file extension for Family Tree Maker to recognize that the file is a backup file.

9. Click on **OK**. The Change filename or directory window will close.

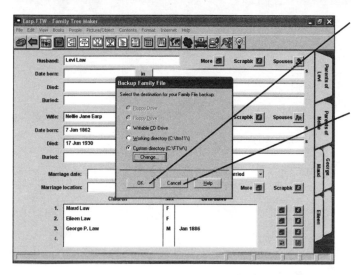

10a. Click on **OK**. The Backup family file dialog box will close and Family Tree Maker will save the backup file.

OR

10b. Click on **Cancel**. The Backup family file dialog box will close and Family Tree Maker will not save the backup file.

22

Working with Family Tree Maker Preferences

Family Tree Maker is a powerful program that offers many features and options. Better still, Family Tree Maker allows you, the user, to define your preferences for many of the screens and more common activities. In this chapter, you'll learn how to:

- Establish Fastfields

- Select screen labels for the Family Page

- Protect Information on living relatives before sharing data

- Select FamilyFinder preferences

- Work with cue card preferences

- Customize the toolbar buttons

- Learn about the number of individuals in your database

Changing Family Tree Maker Preferences

There are many preferences in Family Tree Maker, i.e. the feel of the program and the way it responds to certain input, that can be changed or selected so that each time you use the program you get the same look or response.

Working with the Edit Options

One of the reasons why people use software programs in their genealogy research is to cut down on duplication. One of the ways Family Tree Maker aids in this is through the Fastfields, which is just one of the entry settings found in the Edit tab.

1. Click on **File**. The File menu will appear.

2. Click on **Preferences**. The Preferences dialog box will open.

TIP

The default setting is to have all of the Fastfields turned on. To turn any of them off, simply click on the check box next to the one that you want to turn off. If there is no check mark in the box, then the Fastfield has been turned off.

3. Check or uncheck any of the desired **Fastfield options**.

4. Click on **OK**. The changes will be saved and the Preferences dialog box will close.

NOTE

Fastfields are designed so that you can begin typing the first few letters of a place name, for instance, and Family Tree Maker will supply you with a previously entered place that shares the same first few letters. If it is the place you want, press the Tab key to accept that place and move the cursor. If it isn't the place you want, continue typing the place name.

TIP

If you find that a Fastfield word is misspelled or you want to get rid of it, click on the Trash can next to the word. This will delete it from the Fastfield. You can then type in the correct word.

Establishing File Protection and Backup

Family Tree Maker allows you to determine whether or not it should automatically back up your Family File and if it should help you protect the names of Family Files. Be sure to reopen the Preferences dialog box under the File menu before continuing.

1. Click on **File Protection & Backup**. The File Protection & Backup options will be brought to the front of the Preferences dialog box.

2. Click on the **Automatically back up Family File at shutdown** checkbox. The checkbox will be disabled.

3. Click on the **Don't allow new files with same filename as existing ones** checkbox. The checkbox will be disabled.

TIP

It is a good idea to leave both of these options turned on, that is with the check mark in the checkbox. This not only creates a backup of your file when exiting the program but prevents you from overwriting an existing Family File when creating a new one.

Establishing Some Interface Preferences

The Help & Setup options allow you to change the look and feel of the main screens in which you work when adding or viewing your ancestors in Family Tree Maker.

1. Click on **Help & Setup**. The Help & Setup options will be brought to the front of the Preferences dialog box.

NOTE

If you prefer not to have the cue cards or yellow bubble help boxes appear, you can turn them off by clicking on the check boxes. This is also where you would turn them back on if you wish to take advantage of the help they offer.

2. Click on the **down arrow** for the background color. The list of color choices will appear.

3. Click on the **color** you want for the background in the Family Page. The color will be selected.

NOTE

Family Tree Maker will not change the background color of the Family Page until you have exited the program and gone back in.

Selecting Family Page Labels

The default setting for the Family Page and the reports is Husband and Wife. Some people do not like to use these terms, instead preferring something like Father and Mother. Family Tree Maker allows you to make changes to these labels.

1. Click on **Labels, Titles & LDS**. The Labels, Titles & LDS options will be brought to the front of the Preferences dialog box.

2. Change the **label** for the Husband or Wife. The label will be changed and will show itself on the Family Page.

TIP

If you want to track LDS events, including having two additional reports to show incomplete individual and marriage ordinances, then turn on the Add LDS formats to Reports check box. This will make some changes to your reports, especially the format of the family group sheet to accommodate the LDS dates.

NOTE

If you wish to return labels to the default settings click on the Use Defaults button and the labels will be returned to the defaults, including Husband and Wife for the Family Page.

Establishing Picture Quality

Family Tree Maker has established default settings when it comes to the quality of the images to be printed in the reports and trees. While the defaults are usually suitable, there are times when you may want to see what changing the settings offers in the quality of the output.

1. Click on **Picture Quality**. The Picture Quality options will be brought to the front of the Preferences dialog box.

2. Click on the **compression** radio button for the amount of compression you want. The compression option will be selected.

TIP

The Resolution radio button is only available when using a Kodak Photo CD. It allows you to select the size of the pictures. Generally speaking, the higher the resolution the clearer the picture will be. However, the higher the resolution the larger the file size of the picture will be as well.

NOTE

You may want to experiment with the compression to see how it changes the picture. Print a single picture using different compression options. Remember that the less compression used the larger the picture file will be on your computer.

Tracking Reference Numbers

There are some researchers who prefer to see the reference numbers for those individuals entered in the Family File. At one time genealogy programs relied on these numbers to find someone in the database. Today's software uses names, though some researchers prefer to have the reference numbers available. They do offer a way of tracking individuals with the same name who may have little else to distinguish them from others in the Family File with the same name.

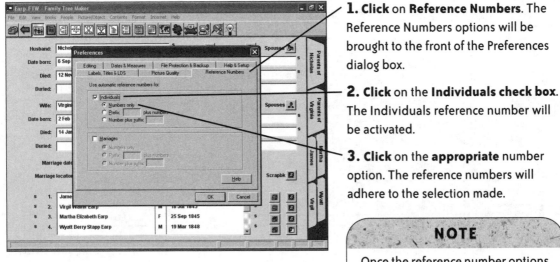

1. Click on **Reference Numbers**. The Reference Numbers options will be brought to the front of the Preferences dialog box.

2. Click on the **Individuals check box**. The Individuals reference number will be activated.

3. Click on the **appropriate** number option. The reference numbers will adhere to the selection made.

> **NOTE**
>
> Once the reference number options have been selected, you will need to remember to turn on the display options in the appropriate reports to view the numbers.

4. Click on **OK**. The Preferences dialog box will close and the changes made will take effect.

Protecting Privacy

There has been much concern of late, especially in the genealogical community, about the sharing of personal information on living individuals. Family Tree Maker allows you to privatize this information.

1. Click on **File**. The File menu will appear.

2. Click on **Privatize File**. The Privatize Information message box will open.

3a. Click on **Yes**. The message box will close and the Family File will be privatized.

OR

3b. Click on **No**. The message box will close and the Family File will not be privatized.

Customizing the Toolbar

While Family Tree Maker has set up the toolbar with those options that are considered the most popular, it is possible that you might rely more heavily on something not currently available on the toolbar. You can remove buttons, rearrange their order, and add new ones.

1. Click on **File**. The File menu will appear.

2. Click on **Preferences**. The Preferences dialog box will open.

3. Click on **Help & Setup**. The Help & Setup options will be brought to the front of the Preferences dialog box.

4. Click on **Customize Toolbar**. The Customize Toolbar dialog box will open.

5. Click on an **available item**. The item will be selected.

6. Click on the **> button**. The item will be added to the bottom of the Your toolbar Contains list.

7. Click on the **newly added item** in the Your toolbar Contains list. The item will be selected.

8. Click on the **Move Up button**. The item will move up in the Your toolbar Contains list.

NOTE

The items that you move up and down in the Your toolbar Contains list will be moved to the left or right on the toolbar once you have finished making changes.

9. Click on **OK**. The Customize Toolbar dialog box will close and the toolbar will be updated.

10. Click on **OK**. The Preferences dialog box will close.

Family File Statistics

Family Tree Maker keeps track of a number of different items in your family file including number of individuals and the number of marriages. You can also have Family Tree Maker calculate how many surnames there are in the database as well as the total number of generations. Most people just like to know how many people they have in the database.

1. Click on **Help**. The Help menu will appear.

2. Click on **Family File Statistics**. The Family File Statistics dialog box will open.

3. Click on **Calculate**. The number of Generations in the database will be displayed.

4. Click on **Calculate**. The number of different Surnames in the database will be displayed.

> **NOTE**
>
> In addition to the number of individuals and marriages in the database, the Family File Statistics dialog box also shows you the average lifespan and the earliest birth date found in the family file.

5. **Click** on **Close**. The Family File Statistics dialog box will close.

23

Enhancing Your Family History Book

While the Book feature in Family Tree Maker offers many valuable options for creating a family history book, it is also possible to add additional reports and outside material to your book. In this chapter, you'll learn how to:

- Select additional reports in advance
- Use the Save View As option
- Rename the items in the Outline view
- Add place holders for outside material
- Add additional items to a previously saved book

Preparing Reports in Advance

People often do not think about the reports that they would like to include in their book until they are actually in the Books window. However, you can create specific reports ahead of time and then incorporate them into one or all of your books.

1. Press the **F2 key**. The Index of Individuals dialog box will open.

2. Type part of the **name** of the individual you want for the report. The highlight bar will move to the first person whose name contains those letters.

3. Click on the **individual** you want to select. That person will be highlighted.

4. Click on **OK**. The Index of Individuals dialog box will close.

Selecting and Formatting Reports

You must first decide the goal of these additional reports. For instance, do you want a chapter of Family Group Sheets on each family that will be found in the narrative section of the book?

1. Click on the **Family Group Sheet button**. The Family Group Sheet for the individual you selected will appear.

TIP

If you are going to create a chapter of Family Group Sheets in your book, you might want to change the generic "Family Group Sheet" title on each Family Group Sheet Report you generate to better represent who is included in the report.

2. Click on **Contents**. The Contents menu will appear.

3. Click on **Title & Footnote**. The Title & Footnote for Family Group Sheet dialog box will open.

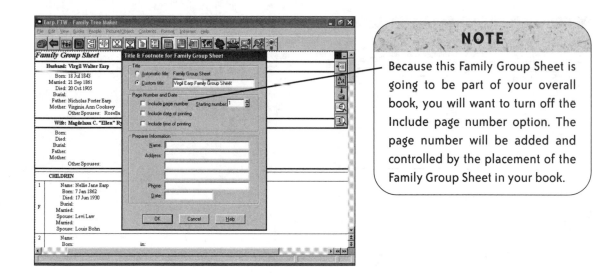

4. Click on the **Custom title radio button**. The cursor will move to the Custom title field.

5. Type the **new title** for the Family Group Sheet.

TIP

You might want to use the name of the father as your title if you will be creating many Family Group Sheets for your book.

NOTE

Because this Family Group Sheet is going to be part of your overall book, you will want to turn off the Include page number option. The page number will be added and controlled by the placement of the Family Group Sheet in your book.

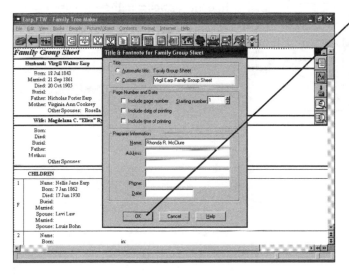

6. Click in the **Name field**. The cursor will move to the Name field.

7. Type the **name** of the preparer and **press** the **Tab key**. The cursor will move to the first Address field.

TIP

Because this is going to be included in your book, you might not want to include your address at the bottom of each page. However, don't overlook this valuable information when printing out Family Group Sheets to share with other researchers.

NOTE

The preparer name, address, and phone number will print at the bottom of the Family Group Sheet. However, the date will print at the top, opposite the title.

8. Click on **OK**. The Title & Footnote for Family Group Sheet dialog box will close and the changes will take effect on the Family Group Sheet Report that is displayed.

Using the Save View As Option

Once you have your report just the way you want it, you can save the report and use it later in any of your books.

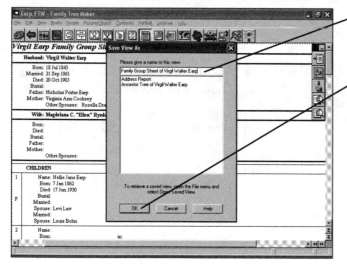

1. Click on **File**. The File menu will appear.

2. Click on **Save Family Group Sheet As**. The Save View As dialog box will open.

> **NOTE**
>
> This File menu option will change according to the report you have open.

3. Type the **name** of the report. The default name will be changed for the title that appears in the View list.

4. Click on **OK**. The Save View As dialog box will close.

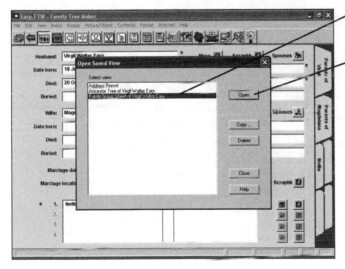

5. Click on the appropriate **view**. The view will be highlighted.

6. Click on the **Open button**. The Open Saved View dialog box will close and the selected Report view will open.

Renaming Outline Items

While Family Tree Maker has default names for all of the reports, you are not required to use those titles.

1. Click on **Books**. The Books menu will appear.

2. Click on **Open Book**. The Open Book dialog box will open.

3. Click on the appropriate **book**. The book will be highlighted.

4. Click on **OK**. The Open Book dialog box will close and the Book view will open.

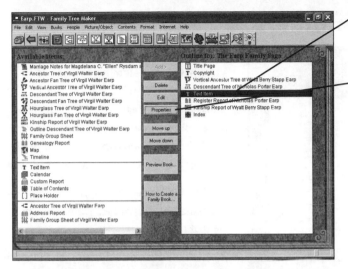

5. Click on the appropriate **item** in the Outline for list. The item will be highlighted.

6. Click on the **Properties button**. The Item Properties dialog box will open.

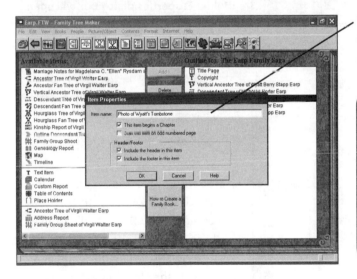

7. Type the new **name** in the Item name field. This will replace the old item name.

TIP

You can also set up chapter beginnings and control whether or not the report begins on an odd-numbered page. If the report is going to begin a new chapter, you might want to think about beginning that chapter on an odd-numbered page, which is the standard in most books.

8. Click on **OK**. The Item Properties dialog box will close and the item name will change in the Outline for list.

Adding Place Holders

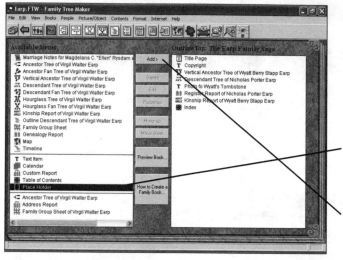

Many times you will want to incorporate a family story created in another program, or some special hand-drawn charts or photo pages in your book. The place holder allows you to reserve a set number of pages anywhere in your book to insert these other items after printing.

1. Click on **Place Holder** in the Available items list. Place Holder will be highlighted.

2. Click on the **Add> button**. The Place Holder Properties dialog box will open.

3. Type the **name** of the item in the Item name field. The words "Place Holder" will be replaced with the name you have typed.

TIP

You will want to give the place holder a descriptive name so that you can easily recall what will go into those pages. This item name will be displayed in the Outline for list and, unlike in the other reports, you cannot open this item to refresh your memory about what is in it.

---

4. Click on the **up or down arrows** to select the number of pages to hold.

5. Click on **OK**. The Place Holder Properties dialog box will close.

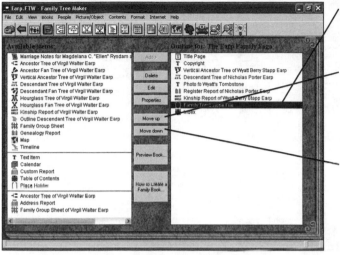

6. Click on the **place holder item** in the Outline for list. The place holder item will be highlighted.

7a. Click on the **Move up button**. The place holder item will be moved up in the Outline for list.

OR

7b. Click on the **Move down button**. The place holder item will be moved down in the Outline for list.

NOTE

Don't forget that the Index must be the last item in the Outline for list. In fact, if you try to move something below it, Family Tree Maker will open a message box explaining that you cannot do that.

Adding to a Book

While you may have already created a book and saved it, this does not mean you can't build on that book. Family Tree Maker allows you to add additional reports at a later date to any previously saved book.

Adding Saved Reports to Books

You can incorporate Save View As reports into any book at any time. Once you have created them, they are available in any Books view, new or previously saved.

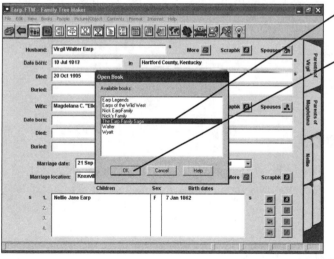

1. Click on **Books**. The Books menu will appear.

2. Click on **Open Book**. The Open Book dialog box will open.

3. Click on the appropriate **book**. The book will be highlighted.

4. Click on **OK**. The Open Book dialog box will close and the Book view will open.

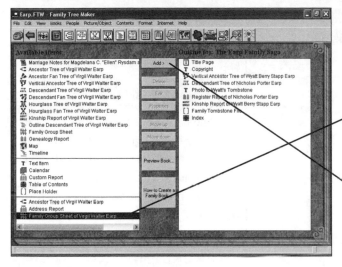

5. Click on the appropriate **saved report** from the Available items list. The report will be highlighted.

6. Click on the **Add> button**. The report will be added to the Outline for list.

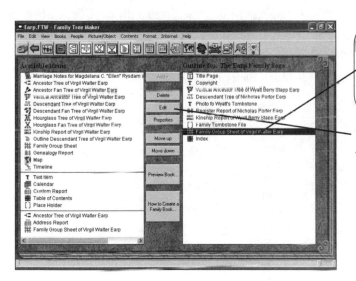

7. Click on the **Edit button**. The report will open for editing.

8. Click on the **Go Back button** when you are done editing the report. You will be returned to the Books view.

NOTE

You can see the page number that has been assigned based on where the report is presently located in the book. This number will change if the report is moved up or down in the Outline for list in the Books view.

Adding Reports about Other Individuals

When a book is first created, it relies on the reports of the selected individual. Once a book has been saved, though, you can add additional reports about other people, giving you a lot of flexibility in your book and its layout.

1. Press the **F2 key**. The Index of Individuals dialog box will open.

2. Click on the desired **individual**. The individual will be highlighted.

3. Click on **OK**. The Index of Individuals dialog box will close and the Available items list in the Books view will reflect the change in individuals.

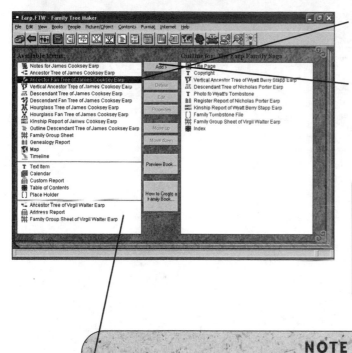

4. Click on the appropriate **item** in the Available items list. That item will be highlighted.

5. Click on the **Add> button**. The selected item will be added to the bottom of the Outline for list, just above the Index item.

TIP

If you click on the selected item in the Outline for list, you can use the various buttons to reposition the item, edit it, or change its properties. It is now a part of the book unless you elect to delete it.

NOTE

Notice that while you changed the focus of the individual in the Available items list, your saved reports are still available.

Adding Notes to Books

If you have spent time adding notes about the individuals in your Family File, there will be times when you will want to include the notes in your book, especially when sharing with family members.

1. Click on **Books**. The Books menu will appear.

2. Click on **Open Book**. The Open Book dialog box will open.

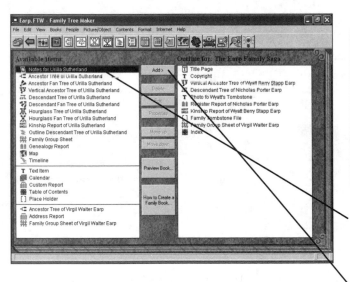

3. Click on the appropriate **book**. The book will be highlighted.

4. Click on **OK**. The Open Book dialog box will close and the Book view will open.

TIP

The Notes for item will only appear in the Available Items list if the individual selected has notes. Remember if the person for whom the available items is not the person you want, you can access the Index of Individuals using the F2 key.

5. Click on **Notes for** in the Available items list. The Notes for item will be selected.

6. Click on the **Add> button**. A message box will appear.

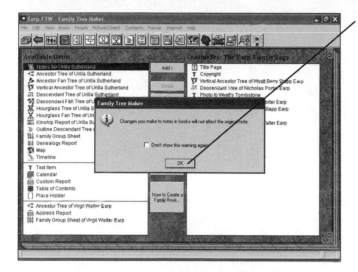

7. Click on **OK**. The message box will close and the Notes will be added to the Outline for list of items to be included in the book.

NOTE

Once in the Outline, the notes can be edited as appropriate for the book. Remember that any changes made at this stage, will not affect your notes in the More About Notes window for that individual or marriage.

You have not only been introduced to Family Tree Maker, but you have been shown many of the advanced features and some tricks to get the most out of the program. Sharing your genealogy online or in print is limited only by your own possibilities. Happy ancestor hunting.

Appendixes

Appendix A
Installing Family Tree Maker .395

Appendix B
Using Keyboard Shortcuts 401

Glossary 405
Index 411
About the Author 419

A

Installing Family Tree Maker

Family Tree Maker has been designed to be easy to install. In this first appendix, you'll learn how to:

- Install Family Tree Maker Version 11 on your computer

- Choose the options you want to install

- Uninstall Family Tree Maker from your computer

Installing Family Tree Maker Version 11

Most computers use an autorun feature when you put a new program CD into your CD-ROM drive—the CD begins to run without your having to do anything.

1. Insert the **Family Tree Maker 10 CD-ROM** into your computer's CD-ROM drive. The automatic installer will start.

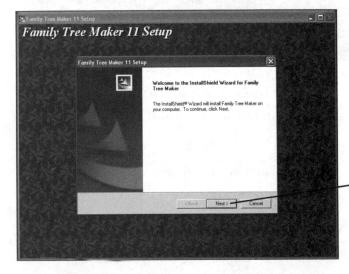

NOTE

Family Tree Maker's installer will encourage you to close any programs you have running at the time you begin to install Family Tree Maker 11. (This is a good idea whenever you are installing software.)

2. Click on **Next** after you have closed all other open programs. The Access Your Online Data dialog box will open.

3. Click on **Next**. The Software License Agreement dialog box will open.

4. Read the **License Agreement**.

5. Click on **Yes**. The Choose Destination Location dialog box will open.

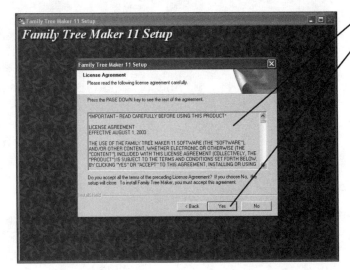

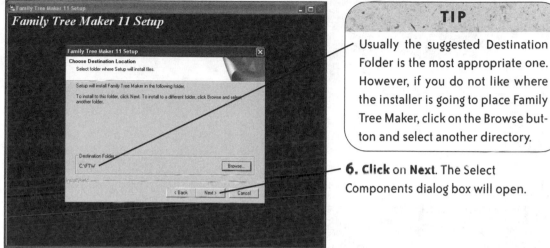

TIP

Usually the suggested Destination Folder is the most appropriate one. However, if you do not like where the installer is going to place Family Tree Maker, click on the Browse button and select another directory.

6. Click on **Next**. The Select Components dialog box will open.

Choosing Components

Family Tree Maker allows you to decide which of the available components you want to install.

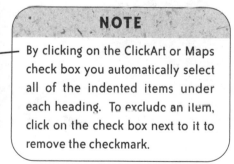

1. Click on the **check box** next to the components you want to install. A check mark will appear next to each component you select.

NOTE

By clicking on the ClickArt or Maps check box you automatically select all of the indented items under each heading. To exclude an item, click on the check box next to it to remove the checkmark.

2. Click on **Next**. The Select Components dialog box will close and Family Tree Maker will begin to install.

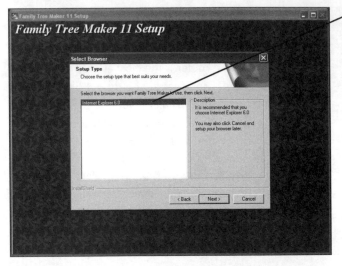

3. Select your **browser** and then **click** on **Next**. The final screen will appear.

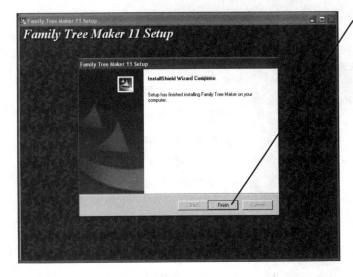

4. Click on the **Finish button** to complete the installation process.

Uninstalling Family Tree Maker

There might come a time when you need to remove Family Tree Maker from your computer. Family Tree Maker has included an uninstall option.

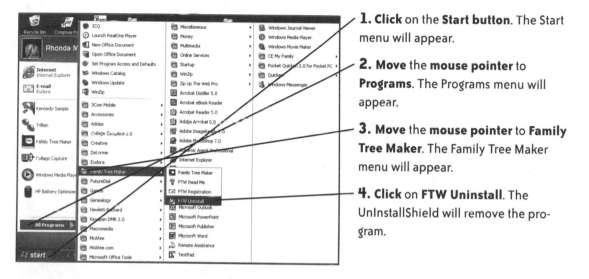

1. Click on the **Start button**. The Start menu will appear.

2. Move the **mouse pointer** to **Programs**. The Programs menu will appear.

3. Move the **mouse pointer** to **Family Tree Maker**. The Family Tree Maker menu will appear.

4. Click on **FTW Uninstall**. The UnInstallShield will remove the program.

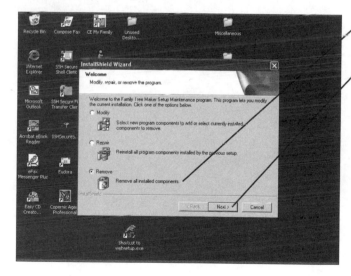

5. Click on **Remove**. The radio button will move to the Remove selection.

6. Click on **Next**. The InstallShield will verify you want to remove the program. Answering no will cancel the InstallShield.

NOTE

On occasion you may find it necessary to reinstall the program if you are having problems. To do this make sure the radio button is next to Repair. When you wish to add clip art or maps that you did not install originally, select the Modify option to make these changes.

B Using Keyboard Shortcuts

Many people prefer not to have to reach for the mouse when they're entering information. Keyboard shortcuts allow you to accomplish many of the tasks for which you would normally need to use the mouse. Throughout the book your attention has been called to some of the keyboard shortcuts included in this appendix, but here you can see the information at a glance. In this appendix, you'll learn how to:

- Use the keyboard shortcuts found in Family Tree Maker

- Use keyboard combinations in text windows

Learning the Keyboard Shortcuts

While it might seem like you will never remember the shortcuts, you will find that the shortcut commands become second nature as you spend more time in Family Tree Maker.

Getting Help

Although you can always open the Help menu, you can use the keyboard shortcuts shown in the following table to get to the help you need more quickly.

To execute this command	Do this
Use Family Tree Maker Help	Press the F1 key
Use the What's This? Button	Press the Shift and F1 keys at the same time (Shift+F1)

Working in Family Tree Maker

The following table puts the keyboard shortcuts related to Family Tree Maker commands together for an easy reference.

To execute this command	Do this
Create a new Family File	Press Ctrl+N
Open a different Family File	Press Ctrl+O
Print a report	Press Ctrl+P
Undo/Redo	Press Ctrl+Z
Create a new To-Do item	Press Ctrl+T
Access the Index of Individuals	Press F2
View a source	Press Ctrl+S
Open the Other Spouses dialog box	Press F3
Access a More About Picture window	Press Ctrl+M
Get Family File status	Press Alt+F1
Get system information	Press Ctrl+F1
Exit Family Tree Maker	Press Alt+F4

Working with Text

While most of the entries in Family Tree Maker are made in fields, there are a number of text windows for typing notes. The following tables contain some shortcuts you might find useful when working in the text windows.

Selecting Text

The first step in manipulating your text is to select it. The following table offers some keyboard combinations for selecting a letter, a word, a line, or more.

To execute this command	Do this
Highlight the character to the right of the insertion point	Press Shift+Right Arrow
Highlight the character to the left of the insertion point	Press Shift+Left Arrow
Highlight an entire word to the right of the insertion point	Press Ctrl+Shift+Right Arrow
Highlight an entire word to the left of the insertion point	Press Ctrl+Shift+Left Arrow
Highlight an entire line	Press Shift+End
Highlight a paragraph one line at a time	Press Shift+Down Arrow for each line of the paragraph
Highlight all lines above the insertion point	Press Ctrl+Shift+Home

Copying and Pasting Text and Individuals

After you select the text or individual(s) you want to work with, you might want to remove it or copy it for placement elsewhere. The following table contains the keyboard combinations you need to manipulate selected text or information about individuals.

If you type this	Family Tree Maker will find this
Copy text	Press Ctrl+C
Cut text	Press Ctrl+X
Paste text	Press Ctrl+V
Delete text	Press Del
Copy Selected Individual	Press Ctrl+I
Copy All individuals in Family Page	Press Ctrl+A

Glossary

Ahnentafel. German for *ancestor table*. In addition to being a chart, it also refers to a genealogical numbering system.

Ancestor. A person from whom one descends.

Ancestor Tree. Also known as a *Pedigree Chart*, this chart begins with a specific individual and displays direct lineage of all of the individual's ancestors.

Annotation. Personal notes or comments that either explain or critique. Family Tree Maker employs annotations in the Bibliography Report.

Bibliography. A report that shows a list of sources used to compile the information included in the genealogy. The sources follow an accepted format, which Family Tree Maker has built into the program.

BMP. Bitmap. A file format for graphics.

Book. In Family Tree Maker, a compilation of reports generated for a family or an individual, including family trees, miscellaneous reports, stories, photos, a table of contents, and an index.

Brightness. An adjustment that can be made to scanned images to make the image lighter or darker.

Browser. See *Web browser*.

Case Sensitive. Differentiating between uppercase and lowercase characters.

Citation. The accepted notation of the source of information.

Cite. The act of making note of the proof that supports a conclusion or claimed fact in the genealogy.

Clipboard. A memory feature of the Windows environment that allows a person to copy or cut text or graphics from one document and paste them into another.

Contrast. An adjustment made to scanned images that causes the image to brighten or dim.

Compression. A setting that determines the quality of the images and the size of the image files you are working with in Family Tree Maker that will be put in your scrapbook and printed out on trees and reports.

CSV. Comma Separated Value(s). A file that separates data by comma which then allows importing into a spreadsheet program.

Cue Cards. The pop-up help windows that appear when you move from screen to screen in Family Tree Maker. They can be turned on or off using the system preferences.

Descendant. A person who descends lineally from another.

Descendant Tree. A chart that lists an individual and his or her descendants.

Endnotes. Source citations and explanatory notes that appear at the end of a document, specifically a tree or report.

Export. To transfer data from one computer to another or from one computer program to another.

Family File. Family Tree Maker's name for the database that contains the information about your lineage.

FamilyFinder Index. A genealogical list containing more than 750 million names that is included in Family Tree Maker's CDs and online.

Family Group Sheet. A form that displays information on a single, complete family unit.

Family Page. The main screen in Family Tree Maker, into which you enter information about a particular individual and family.

Fastfields. Family Tree Maker remembers the names of the last 50 locations you have typed in so that as you begin to type in a place in a new location field, Family Tree Maker shows you possible matches based on the letters you have typed up to that point.

Format. One of Family Tree Maker's options for developing the style and look of reports and trees.

GEDCOM. GEnealogical Data COMmunication. A standard designed by the Family History Department of the Church of Jesus Christ of Latter-Day Saints for transferring data between different genealogy software packages.

Genealogy Report. A narrative style report that details a family through one or more generations and includes basic facts about each member in addition to biographical information that was entered through Family Tree Maker.

Generation. The period of time between the birth of one group of individuals and the next—usually about 25 to 33 years.

GIF. Graphic Interchange Format. A graphic file format that is widely used in webpage documents.

Given Name. The first name (and middle name) given to a child at birth or at his or her baptism. Also known as a *Christian name*.

Home Page. The main page of a website.

Hourglass Tree. A chart showing both the ancestors and the descendants of a selected individual. When printed, the tree resembles an hourglass because the ancestors spread out above the selected individual and the descendants spread out below.

HTML. Hypertext Markup Language. The standard language for creating and formatting webpages.

Import. To bring into a program a file that was created using another program.

Individual Facts Card. A multi-tabbed dialog box that allows you easy access to all of the personal information (corresponding to the Family Page and More About pages) for a specific individual.

Inline Notes. The sources that appear within the text as opposed to at the bottom or end of a page in Family Tree Maker's Genealogy Reports.

Kinship. In genealogy, this refers to the relationship between one individual and any or all of his or her relatives. This can be displayed through the Kinship Report in Family Tree Maker.

JPEG. Joint Photographic Expert Group. Graphics that use the .jpg extension include a compression technique that reduces the size of the graphics file.

Maternal Ancestor. An ancestor on the mother's side of the family.

Merge. The ability in Family Tree Maker to take the information of two individuals who appear to be the same person and combine them into a single individual in the Family File.

NGSQ. *National Genealogical Society Quarterly*. A periodical published by that society. Also refers to the NGS Quarterly numbering system offered in descending genealogy reports.

OLE. Object Linking and Embedding. A technology that allows you to create items in one program and place them in another, including video clips, still images, pictures, word-processing files, and spreadsheet files.

Outline Descendant Tree. A chart that shows in an indented outline format an individual's children, grandchildren, great-grandchildren, and so on through the generations.

Paternal Ancestor. An ancestor on the father's side of the family.

PDF. Portable Document Format. A file format that retains printer formatting so that when it is opened it looks as it would if on the printed page. Requires Adobe Acrobat Reader to open and view a file that ends in the .PDF extension.

Pedigree Chart. A chart that shows the direct ancestors of an individual. Known in Family Tree Maker as an *Ancestor Tree*.

Preferred. A term Family Tree Maker uses in reference to parents, spouses, or duplicate events, meaning that you want to see that selection first or have it displayed in trees and reports.

Primary Individual. The main individual in any of the Family Tree Maker charts or reports.

Red-Eye Removal. The method of removing the red, or hollow, look of eyes from flash photographs that have been digitized.

Register. Refers to the descending genealogy format used by the New England Historic Genealogical Society. This also refers to their periodical by the same name.

Reports. Any of a number of standard and custom displays in various formats that Family Tree Maker can create.

Research Journal. A record used by genealogists to keep track of their research findings and tasks to be accomplished.

Resolution. In Family Tree Maker an option allowed when working with Kodak Photo CD files that allows you to increase the size of a picture, thus making it a clearer picture.

Re-Writable CD-ROM. A CD-ROM drive that allows you to save files to a CD-RW disc, a disc designed to be used like a floppy disc and to which you can write to more than once (different from a Writable CD-ROM).

RTF. Rich Text Format. A cross-platform, cross-application text document format. It retains some of the formatting information that is supported by many word processors.

Saturation. The amount of color in each pixel of an image. When the saturation is high, the image shows bright, vivid colors. When the saturation is low, the picture may look black and white.

Scrapbooks. The term used by Family Tree Maker for the collections of photographs, images, video, sound, and OLE objects that can be stored for each individual and marriage in the Family File.

Siblings. Children of the same parents.

Source. The record, such as a book, an e-mail message, or an interview, from which specific information was obtained.

Spouse. The person to whom another person is married.

Surname. The family name or last name of an individual.

Threshold. As used in the Red-Eye Removal Dialog box, the minimum degree of redness for the pixels to be fixed.

Tree. The term Family Tree Maker uses to refer to its various charts. See *Ancestor Tree*, *Descendant Tree*, and *Outline Descendant Tree*.

URL. Uniform Resource Locator. The address used by a Web browser to locate a page on the Web.

User Home Page. The section of Genealogy.com where individual researcher's data is shared on the Web.

WAV. Windows Audio Visual. The sound files that work with Media Player and Sound Recorder.

Web browser. The software that lets you access pages on the Web. The browser reads the HTML code and converts it to the pictures, colors, menu options, and overall design that you view on your monitor.

Webpage. An Internet document that is written using a scripting language such as HTML.

Website. A location on the Internet maintained by a single individual, company, or entity that provides information, graphics, and other items.

Wizard. A step-by-step interactive process in Family Tree Maker that gathers information from you in an easy manner. Wizards are used to introduce you to new processes, such as adding information on people or creating a family history webpage.

World Family Tree (WFT) Project. A multi-volume CD and online collection created by Genealogy.com from the genealogies submitted electronically by family history enthusiasts and indexed in the FamilyFinder Index.

World Wide Web. A graphical interface that is composed of Internet sites that provide researchers with access to documents and other files.

Writable CD-ROM. A CD-ROM drive that allows you to save files to a CD-R disc, a disc designed to be used like a floppy disc.

Index

A

addresses
>creating Address Reports, 228–29
>entering, 89–90

ages, calculating, 335–36

Ahnentafel format reports, 249–50

aliases, 94

All-in-One Trees
>changing the text font, 238–39
>creating, 209
>customizing borders and backgrounds, 240
>in family history books, 289
>printing, 242–43
>pruning the display, 210–11
>saving in PDF format, 244
>setting the display size, 210
>using templates to enhance, 241–42
>*See also* Ancestor Trees; Descendant Trees; Hourglass Trees; InterneTrees

Alternate Facts Reports, 255–56

Ancestor Trees
>changing the text font, 238–39
>creating a Fan Chart, 194–95
>creating a Pedigree Chart, 195–97
>creating a Vertical Ancestor Tree, 198–200
>customizing a Pedigree Chart, 197–98
>customizing borders and backgrounds, 240
>excluding relationship information from, 96
>in family history books, 289
>formats for displaying information, 23–24
>including siblings on, 200–201
>printing, 242–43
>saving in PDF format, 244

>sharing a Standard Pedigree Tree, 202–3
>using templates to enhance, 241–42
>*See also* All-in-One Trees; Descendant Trees; Hourglass Trees; InterneTrees

B

backing up files, 364

Bibliography Reports, 257–58

Birthday Reports, 229–30

births, entering information about, 8–9

C

children
>adding, 37–38
>adding an additional child, 55–57
>adding another set of parents, 51–55
>adding siblings, 50–51
>detaching a child from the wrong parents, 176–78
>linking a child to parents, 174–76
>moving a child, 57–60
>moving a child to the primary individual position, 43
>sorting the order of, 61

closing Family Tree Maker, 28

Copy and Paste function, 27–28

corrections, making. *See* deleting people; duplicates, fixing; family files; marriages; relationships; spelling, checking

Cue Cards, opening/turning off, 16
Custom Reports
    adding items to, 218–19
    adjusting column widths, 224
    choosing individuals to include, 219–20
    exporting, 226
    formatting, 222–23
    removing individuals, 221–22
    sorting, 225
Cut and Paste function, 27–28

D

dates
    calculating, 335–36
    changing the default format for, 33–35
    entering, 31–32
    setting the cutoff for double dating, 34
deaths, entering information about, 9
deleting people
    groups of people, 164–66
    permanency of, 166
    single persons, 163
Descendant Trees
    adding a background image on, 213–15
    changing the text font, 238–39
    customizing borders and backgrounds, 240
    emphasizing relationships on, 211–13
    in family history books, 289
    formats for displaying information, 25
    outline format, 208
    printing, 242–43
    saving in PDF format, 244
    standard format, 206–7
    using templates to enhance, 241–42
    See also All-in-One Trees; Ancestor Trees;
        Hourglass Trees; InterneTrees
dialog boxes, 16
documentation. *See* sources
Documented Events Reports, 258–59
double dating, 34
duplicates, fixing
    undoing merges, 186, 188
    using the Merge All Duplicate Individuals func-
        tion, 181–86
    using the Merge Specific Individuals menu
        option, 186–88

E

events
    entering, 31–33
    See also More About Facts window
exiting Family Tree Maker, 28

F

facts. *See* More About Facts window; Individual Facts
    Cards
Family Files
    backing up, 356–59
    bypassing the wizard and beginning directly in
        the Family Page, 10–12
    checking for data entry errors, 166–68
    importing GEDCOM files into existing, 344–48
    naming, 5
    opening GEDCOM files as new, 349–51
    sharing complete files as GEDCOM files, 338–40
    sharing partial files as GEDCOM files, 340–44
    tracking statistics in, 372–73
    using the Data Errors Report to locate and cor-
        rect errors, 171–72
    using the file history list to open two files simul-
        taneously, 353–55
    using the Find Error command to locate and cor-
        rect errors, 168–70
    using the Open Family File option to open two
        files simultaneously, 352–53
    using the wizard to create, 5–10
FamilyFinder Searches
    initiating a search, 152–53
    viewing a report, 154–55
family history books
    adding notes to, 389–91
    adding page breaks, 295
    adding reports about other individuals to previ-
        ously created books, 388–89
    adding saved reports to previously created
        books, 385–88
    adding trees and reports, 289
    creating an index, 296–97
    creating place holders, 384–85
    on family home pages, 314–15

including text with pictures, 290–92
items to include in, 286
organizing items, 293–94
previewing, 298–99
printing, 299–300
renaming items, 382–83
saving in PDF format, 300–301
saving reports for later use, 380–81
selecting and formatting reports, 376–79
selecting front matter, 287–88
starting a book, 286–87
working with item properties, 294
See also scrapbooks
family home pages
adding an InterneTree, 312–13
adding reports, 309–11
being sensitive to privacy/security issues, 305, 307
deleting, 318–19
getting started with the wizard, 304–6
including a family history book, 314–15
removing a report or book, 316–17
using Create Your Own Home Page, 306–9
Family Page
bypassing the wizard and beginning directly in, 10–12
exploring, 19–22
selecting labels for, 366
Fan Charts
creating, 194–95
Hourglass Tree, 204
Fastfields, 362–63
fields
moving information between, 27–28
using keyboard commands to navigate between, 18–19
Find and Replace feature, 189–90
Find Individual feature
accessing, 144
searching by comment, 151
searching by date, 146–48
searching by location, 148–49
searching by name, 145–46
searching by source, 150

G

GEDCOM files
importing into existing Family Files, 344–48
opening as new Family Files, 349–51
sharing complete Family Files as, 338–40
sharing partial Family Files as, 340–44
Genealogy Style Reports
adding source citations as endnotes, 251–52
adjusting the title and page numbering, 252–53
changing the number of generations, 253
creating Ahnentafel format reports, 249–50
creating NGS Quarterly format reports, 248–49
creating Register format reports, 246–47
including notes and stories, 254
Gregorian calendar, 34

H

home pages. *See* family home pages
Hourglass Trees
changing the text font, 238–39
customizing borders and backgrounds, 240
in family history books, 289
fan format, 204
formats for displaying information, 26
printing, 242–43
saving in PDF format, 244
standard format, 205–6
using templates to enhance, 241–42
See also All-in-One Trees; Ancestor Trees; Descendant Trees; InterneTrees

I

images, attaching to sources, 80–81
Index of Individuals
accessing, 138
quick searching by name, 138
rearranging, 141–43
using the Find feature to search by name, 139–40

Individual Facts Cards
    accessing cards from a Report view, 124–25
    adding a fact, 129–30
    adding a new related individual, 132–33
    adding a note or story, 130–31
    closing, 133–34
    exploring, 22–23
    moving to other related individuals, 131–32
    summary of features, 128
    using the menu option to open, 124
    working in an individual's Family Page *vs.*,
        125–28
InterneTrees, 312–13

J

Julian calendar, 34

K

Kinship Reports
    creating, 227–28
    excluding relationship information from, 96

L

launching Family Tree Maker, 4–5

M

maiden names, 49
mailing lists, 89–90, 228–29
marriages
    correcting, 161–62
    entering approximate dates, 324
    linking married individuals, 178–81
    using the Beginning status field, 324–25
    See also More About Marriage Facts window;
        More About Marriage Notes window; More
        About Marriage window; spouses

master sources. *See* sources
medical information, 91–92
menus
    activating, 14
    executing a command, 15
    grayed-out commands, 14
    keyboard shortcuts for commands, 14
    right-pointing arrows on, 14
merging duplicates. *See* duplicates, fixing
More About Address and Phone(s) window, 89–90
More About Facts window
    accessing, 84
    adding custom facts, 85–86
    adding different names, 86–87
    creating a new fact name, 87–89
    removing a custom fact name, 329–34
More About Lineage window
    accessing, 93
    entering AKA names, 94
    excluding relationship information from
        reports, 96
    recording special relationships, 94–95
More About Marriage Facts window
    adding a marriage fact, 118
    entering a reference number, 117
    getting Family Page to work with, 326–28
    recording ending status, 116–17
    using the Pref'd check box to indicate a pre-
        ferred fact, 119–20
More About Marriage Notes window, 121
More About Marriage window, 116
More About Medical window, 91–92
More About Notes window
    copying notes and stories, 99–100
    copying text from another application, 108–9
    entering notes and stories, 98
    exporting notes and stories, 111–12
    finding a specific word or phrase in, 105–7
    formatting information for printing, 112–13
    importing text files, 109–10
    including source citations, 99
    moving information to a different window,
        101–4
    printing information, 98

N

names
aliases, 94
variant, 86–87
See also surnames
NGS Quarterly format reports, 248–49
notes. *See* family history books; Genealogy Style
Reports; More About Marriage Facts window; More
About Marriage Notes window; More About
Marriage window; More About Notes window;
sources; Individual Facts Cards

O

OLE (Object Linking and Embedding) objects, 268–70

P

parents
adding, 48–50
adding another set of, 51–55
detaching a child from the wrong, 176–78
linking children to, 174–76
surnames of, 48
using maiden names, 49
Pedigree Charts
creating, 195–97
customizing, 197–98
photographs
adjusting color and brightness, 276–77
correcting red eye, 277–79
cropping, 275–76
in family history books, 290–92
inserting in scrapbooks, 265
selecting picture quality, 367
place names, entering, 32–33
preferences
accessing, 362
backing up files and protecting file names, 364
changing the look and feel of screens, 365
Fastfields, 362–63
picture quality, 367

privatizing information on living individuals,
368–69
reference numbers, 368
selecting Family Page labels, 366
toolbar, 370–72
primary individuals
entering, 30
moving a child to the primary individual position, 43
privacy
on family home pages, 305, 307
privatizing information on living individuals,
368–69
protecting file names, 364
Publishing Center. *See* family history books; family
home pages

R

reference numbers, 117, 368
Register format reports, 246–47
relationships
detaching a child from the wrong parents,
176–78
excluding information from reports, 96
linking children to parents, 174–76
linking individuals by marriage, 178–81
recording special, 94–95
Reports. *See* addresses; Alternate Facts Reports;
Bibliography Reports; Birthday Reports; Custom
Reports; Documented Events Reports; family history books; family home pages; Genealogy Style
Reports; Kinship Reports; scrapbooks
Research Journal
accessing, 230
creating a new To-Do item, 231, 235–36
viewing done or not done items, 232
viewing items by categories, 233–34

S

scrapbooks
accessing the Individual Scrapbook window,
264
copying scrapbook objects, 274–75

enhancing photographs, 275–79
including information about scrapbook objects, 270–72
inserting photographs, 265–66
inserting sound clips, 266–68
moving scrapbook objects, 272–73
playing, 281
printing, 282–83
searching for scrapbook objects, 279–80
using OLE (Object Linking and Embedding) objects, 268–70
See also family history books
scroll bars, 17
siblings, adding, 50–51
sound clips, 266–68
sources
attaching images to, 80–81
changing a master source citation, 75–77
creating a master source, 65–68
creating a master source from the Source-Citation dialog box, 73–74
creating a source citation, 71–72
editing master source data, 78–79
fields permitting citation of, 64
importance of citing, 65
including source citations in notes and stories, 99
learning more about source citations, 71
searching for a master source, 79–80
using the Source-Citation dialog box to select a master source, 69–71
spelling, checking
in the entry screens, 158–59
in the More About Notes and More About Marriage Notes windows, 160–61
using global Find and Replace to make corrections, 189–90
spouses
adding, 36–37
adding additional, 38–40
designating the preferred spouse, 40–41
switching to another spouse, 41–42
See also marriages
Standard Pedigree Trees, 202–3
starting Family Tree Maker, 4–5
stories. *See* Genealogy Style Reports; More About Marriage Facts window; More About Marriage Notes window; More About Marriage window; More About Notes window; sources; Individual Facts Cards
surnames
maiden names, 49
of parents, 48
using backward slash marks to identify, 31
See also names

T

toolbar
accessing button names, 15
customizing, 370–72
Trees. *See* All-in-One Trees; Ancestor Trees; Descendant Trees; Hourglass Trees; InterneTrees

V

Vertical Ancestor Trees, 198–200
views
Ancestor Tree, 23–24
Descendant Tree, 25
Family Page, 19–22
Hourglass Tree, 26
Individual Facts Card, 22–23

W

wizards
for creating a family home page, 304–6
for creating a new family file, 5–10

About the Author

Rhonda R. McClure has managed to combine the best of both worlds—computers and genealogy. She has been using a computer to aid in her genealogical research since 1985. She has been teaching genealogists for more than ten years on the benefits of genealogy software, a time-saving addition to their research when understood and used correctly. This is her fourth book on how to use Family Tree Maker.